T0272179

“More than a substance,
plastic is the very idea of
infinite transformation.”

according to Roland Barthes, 1957

„Plastik ist nicht nur eine
Substanz, es ist die Idee
ihrer unendlichen Trans-
formation.“

nach Roland Barthes, 1957

DORIS HIRSCH & BURKHARD JACOB

THE BOOK OF POSSIBILITIES

INSPIRING DESIGN WITH PLEXIGLAS®

reddot edition

CONTENT

From an inspiring material to innovative design

Even today, we take for granted that in the future we will be driven around by driverless cars that also inform and entertain us with their integrated display screens. Or that we will be surrounded by lighting, kitchen aids and household appliances that are as intelligent as they are aesthetic. Every product is representative of a certain period in which it was consciously designed and made.

Materials have always played a decisive role in the development of design. Depending on how materials were used by designers, the function, use or aesthetics of a product also changed. The task for the designer is to find the right material for a certain aesthetic, functional form. The task for the manufacturer is to ensure the quality of the material and to improve its performance and range of applications. So selecting the material is a pivotal moment in the design process.

As a manufacturer of PLEXIGLAS®, we constantly engage in dialog with designers and product developers in order to improve the functional properties of the material. As a result, the diversity and performance of the material today means that it is no longer comparable with the material originally invented. PLEXIGLAS® now marries experience, performance, reliability, emotion and inspiration in a high-tech material that allows for new design forms and technical functions in sophisticated applications in a wide variety of industries.

In the automotive industry, PLEXIGLAS® helps to create an elegant and lasting high-gloss look for car body parts, which additionally make an important contribution to lightweight construction for electric vehicles or also serve as a cover for sensors on self-driving cars. Infotainment, too, is becoming more and more important for self-driving cars: In the interior, displays and decorative panels merge into multi-functional panels with integrated touch and display sensors. Depending on its use, PLEXIGLAS® can create mood lighting or can direct light to where it is needed. As a surface finish, it gives household appliances a long-lasting premium appearance. Consequently, this high-perfomance material is already well established in many of these areas of application, and in others is contributing to creating innovations.

A selection of the many possibilities offered by PLEXIGLAS® can be found in this book. The examples show how innovative design can be inspired by the material itself. This is because the material is much more than the sum of its technical features. This is something that has been rendered tangible for creatives since 2017 by our worldwide "Black & Bright" campaign for PLEXIGLAS® molding compounds with its bold advertising motifs and easy-to-follow workshops. Not least in an exhibition in the Red Dot Design Museum that displayed the branded PMMA and the design possibilities in visual form and which serves as a point of departure for this book.

Over its long history, PLEXIGLAS® has already inspired numerous designers to create extraordinary work. It will continue to do so, for example when integrating new functions into many products used in our everyday lives.

I am sure you will be inspired by reading this book.

Siamak Djafarian

Head of the Molding Compounds division,
the manufacturer of
PLEXIGLAS® molding compounds

Vom inspirierenden Material zum innovativen Design

Es erscheint uns bereits heute wie selbstverständlich, dass wir uns in Zukunft von autonomen Automobilen fahren lassen, die uns nebenbei durch integrierte Displays informieren und unterhalten. Oder auch, dass wir von ebenso ästhetischen wie intelligenten Leuchten, Küchen- und Haushaltsgeräten umgeben sein werden. Dabei steht jedes Produkt für eine bestimmte Zeit, in der es bewusst gestaltet und hergestellt wurde.

In der Entwicklung des Designs haben Werkstoffe immer eine entscheidende Rolle gespielt. Abhängig davon, wie Materialien von Designern für die Gestaltung genutzt wurden, veränderte sich auch die Funktion, der Gebrauch oder die Ästhetik eines Produktes. Für den Designer geht es darum, das passende Material für eine bestimmte ästhetische, funktionelle Form zu finden. Für den Hersteller geht es darum, die Qualität des Werkstoffs zu gewährleisten sowie seine Leistungsfähigkeit und die Anwendungsvielfalt zu verbessern. Daher ist die Auswahl des Materials ein wichtiges Moment im Designprozess.

Als Hersteller von PLEXIGLAS® suchen wir immer wieder den Dialog mit Designern und Produktentwicklern, um die funktionalen Eigenschaften des Materials zu verbessern. Daher ist dieser Werkstoff aufgrund seiner heutigen Vielfalt und Leistungsfähigkeit nicht mehr mit dem Material aus der Zeit seiner Erfindung vergleichbar. PLEXIGLAS® verbindet heute Erfahrung, Leistungsfähigkeit, Verlässlichkeit, Emotion und Inspiration zu einem Hightech-Werkstoff, der neue gestalterische Formen und technische Funktionen in anspruchsvollen Anwendungen in den unterschiedlichsten Branchen erlaubt.

In der Automobilindustrie trägt PLEXIGLAS® zu einem edlen und dauerhaften Hochglanzlook bei Karosserieteilen bei, die darüber hinaus noch einen wichtigen Beitrag zum Leichtbau bei E-Autos leisten oder auch als Abdeckung für Sensoren von autonomen Fahrzeugen dienen. Beim autonomen Fahren erhält auch das Infotainment einen immer höheren Stellenwert: Im Innenraum verschmelzen Displays und Dekorblenden zu multifunktionalen Blenden mit integrierten Touch- und Displaysensoren. Je nach Einsatzbereich sorgt PLEXIGLAS® in der Beleuchtung für stimmungsvolle Momente oder bringt das Licht dorthin, wo es benötigt wird. Als Oberflächenveredelung verleiht es Haushaltsgeräten einen lang anhaltenden Premiumlook. In vielen dieser Anwendungsgebiete ist dieses Hochleistungsmaterial daher längst etabliert – in anderen trägt es dazu bei, Innovationen mitzugestalten.

Eine Auswahl der vielen Möglichkeiten, die PLEXIGLAS® bietet, findet sich auch in diesem Buch wieder. Die Beispiele veranschaulichen, wie innovatives Design durch das Material selbst inspiriert sein kann. Denn der Werkstoff ist weit mehr als die Summe seiner technischen Eigenschaften. Bereits seit 2017 wird dies in unserer weltweiten „Black & Bright"-Kampagne für PLEXIGLAS® Formmassen mit mutigen Anzeigenmotiven und in anschaulichen Workshops für Kreative erlebbar. Nicht zuletzt in einer Ausstellung im Red Dot Design Museum, die das Marken-PMMA und die Gestaltungsmöglichkeiten visualisiert hat und Ausgangspunkt für dieses Buch bildet.

In seiner langen Historie hat PLEXIGLAS® schon viele Designer zu außergewöhnlichen Werken inspiriert und wird dies auch in Zukunft tun. Zum Beispiel, wenn es um die Integration neuer Funktionen in vielen Produkten des täglichen Lebens geht.

Ich bin sicher, die Lektüre dieses Buches wird Sie inspirieren.

Siamak Djafarian

Leiter des Bereichs Molding Compounds, dem Hersteller von PLEXIGLAS® Formmassen

When visions become reality

Every innovative design starts with an initial idea. PLEXIGLAS® comes into play when it is time to turn that creative energy into a real-life project.

Our sheets, rods, tubes and films stand for quality products that meet especially high standards, for example in terms of their longevity. Our branded acrylic glass makes it possible to create everything from architectural façades of lasting impressiveness to striking surfaces in furniture production, lighting elements with homogeneous lighting and evenly illuminated display screens.

Whether for huge commercial aircraft or for small gliders, the materials used in aircraft construction have always been subject to the very highest standards. They have to withstand extreme fluctuations in temperature, protect against UV radiation, be weather-resistant and tough. In addition, they need to be as light as possible, because low fuel consumption through lower weight is an important objective. PLEXIGLAS® helps to keep these developments moving forward.

As one of the world's best-known plastic brands, this material offers varied possibilities for design alongside outstanding functional properties.

Discover the fascinating world of PLEXIGLAS® inside this book.

Martin Krämer

Head of the Acrylic Products division, the manufacturer of PLEXIGLAS® sheets, rods, tubes and films

Wenn Visionen Realität werden

Jedes innovative Design beginnt mit einer ersten Idee. PLEXIGLAS® kommt dann ins Spiel, wenn aus der Schöpferkraft ein reales Projekt werden soll.

Unsere Platten, Stäbe, Rohre und Folien stehen dabei für eine Qualität von Produkten, an die besonders hohe Anforderungen gestellt werden, beispielsweise im Hinblick auf ihre Langlebigkeit. So ermöglicht unser Markenacrylglas dauerhaft beeindruckende Fassaden in der Architektur ebenso wie aufmerksamkeitsstarke Oberflächen im Möbelbau, homogen erstrahlende Elemente in der Beleuchtung oder gleichmäßig ausgeleuchtete Displays.

Ob riesiges Verkehrsflugzeug oder kleiner Segelflieger: Für Materialien im Flugzeugbau gelten seit jeher höchste Anforderungen. Sie müssen extreme Temperaturwechsel aushalten, gegen UV-Strahlung schützen, witterungsbeständig und robust sein – und dazu

noch möglichst wenig wiegen, denn ein wichtiges Ziel dabei ist geringerer Spritverbrauch durch weniger Gewicht. PLEXIGLAS® trägt dazu bei, dass auch diese Entwicklungen immer weiter voranschreiten.

Dieser Werkstoff bietet als eine der bekanntesten Kunststoffmarken der Welt vielfältige Möglichkeiten in der Gestaltung bei zugleich herausragenden Gebrauchseigenschaften.

Entdecken Sie die faszinierende Welt von PLEXIGLAS® auch in diesem Buch!

Martin Krämer

Leiter des Bereichs Acrylic Products, dem Hersteller von PLEXIGLAS® Platten, Stäben, Rohren und Folien

DESIGN ICONS MADE OF PLASTIC

“Plastics have conquered the world without us really noticing.”

according to Klaus Euler, 1959

„Kunststoffe haben die Welt erobert, ohne dass wir es richtig bemerkt haben.“

nach Klaus Euler, 1959

DESIGN ICONS MADE OF PLASTIC

When Richard Escales published the first issue of a new trade magazine called "Kunststoffe" (Plastics) in 1911, neither the word nor the material were known. No-one at the time had any idea what a prominent role plastics would one day play in design and daily life.

Historically, plastics initially only fulfilled the role of an attractive alternative to scarce or increasingly expensive materials. As a chemist, Escales however had a vision that science could one day succeed in developing synthetically manufactured materials that would be superior to natural materials in their functionality and performance, and thus give rise to a new industry – a vision that rapidly became reality, but not one that Escales lived to see.

It is the discoveries and contributions that chemist Hermann Staudinger made to macromolecular chemistry which soon led to the development of the first thermoplastics such as polyvinyl chloride, polystyrene, polymethyl methacrylate, polyamide, polyester or polyurethane. Not only the production and quality of plastics quickly progressed after that, but so did manufacturing and forming processes such as extrusion and injection molding.

From the mid twentieth century onwards, plastic products symbolized a new lifestyle. With the start of the economic boom period after the Second World War, they became the new icons of our culture. Without claiming to offer an exhaustive overview, the objects presented here reflect this transformation and provide a look back on the significance of plastics to design along an imagined trajectory that is more of a formline than a timeline. To this day, they shape our aesthetics and our cultural memory, and suggest that the 21st century will also be a century of plastics.

DESIGNIKONEN AUS KUNSTSTOFF

Als Richard Escales 1911 die erste Ausgabe einer neuen Fachzeitschrift mit dem Titel „Kunststoffe" veröffentlicht, gibt es zuvor weder das Wort noch den Werkstoff, und niemand ahnt zu diesem Zeitpunkt, welche herausragende Rolle die Kunststoffe im Design und in unserer Alltagskultur einmal spielen werden.

Historisch gesehen, erfüllen Kunststoffe anfangs nur die Rolle von Imitationen oder günstigen Surrogaten für knapp oder teuer gewordene Materialien. Als Chemiker hat Escales aber die Vision, dass es der Wissenschaft gelingen könnte, synthetisch herstellbare Werkstoffe zu entwickeln, die natürlichen Werkstoffen in ihrer Funktionalität und Leistung überlegen sind, um darauf eine neue Industrie aufzubauen. Eine Vision, die rasch Wirklichkeit wird, die Escales aber nicht mehr erlebt.

Die Erkenntnisse und Beiträge des Chemikers Hermann Staudinger zur makromolekularen Chemie sind es dann, die schon bald zu den ersten thermoplastischen Kunststoffen wie etwa Polyvinylchlorid, Polystyrol, Polymethylmethacrylat, Polyamid, Polyester oder Polyurethan führen. Nicht nur die Herstellung und Qualität der Kunststoffe entwickelt sich danach rasch weiter, sondern auch die Fertigungs- und Formgebungsverfahren wie beispielsweise die Extrusion oder das Spritzgießen.

Seit Mitte des 20. Jahrhunderts symbolisieren Produkte aus Kunststoff einen neuen Lebensstil und wandeln sich mit Beginn des Wirtschaftswunders zu neuen Ikonen unserer Kultur. Ohne Anspruch auf Vollständigkeit spiegeln die hier ausgewählten Objekte diesen Wandel wider und lassen entlang einer gedachten Achse, die mehr Formenstrahl als Zeitstrahl ist, die Bedeutung der Kunststoffe im Design Revue passieren. Sie prägen bis heute unsere Ästhetik und unser kulturelles Gedächtnis und lassen erahnen, dass auch das 21. Jahrhundert ein Jahrhundert der Kunststoffe sein wird.

1934 [1]

1937 [3]

1937 [2]

PF.

PF – Phenol formaldehyde resins (phenoplastics), invented by Leo Hendrik Baekeland, are among the earliest industrial plastics. The raw materials are phenol and formaldehyde. These duroplastic polymers are created by means of polycondensation. Applications: rigid molded parts for cameras, radios, telephones, and household objects. Famous trademarks: Aramith, Bakelite, and Philite.

PF – Phenol-Formaldehyd-Harze (Phenoplaste), *von Leo Hendrik Baekeland erfunden, zählen zu den ersten industriell erzeugten Kunststoffen. Ausgangsstoffe sind Phenol und Formaldehyd. Durch Polykondensation entstehen die duroplastischen Polymere. Anwendungen: stabile Formteile für Kameras, Radios, Telefone und Haushaltsgegenstände. Bekannte Warenzeichen: Aramith, Bakelit und Philite.*

1940 [5]

1939 [4]

1962 [6]

1. **1934 Baby Brownie,** Eastman Kodak Company, USA, Design: Walter Dorwin Teague
2. **1937 Purma Special,** Thomas De La Rue, UK, Purma Cameras, UK, Design: Raymond Loewy
3. **1937 Radio Nurse,** Zenith Radio Corporation, USA, Design: Isamu Noguchi
4. **1939 Philishave, Type 7730,** Royal Philips, The Netherlands, Design: Alexandre Horowitz
5. **1940 Ducati Microphone,** Ducati, Italy, Design: Gio Ponti
6. **1962 Braun sixtant SM 31,** Braun, Germany, Design: Hans Gugelot, Gerd Alfred Müller

PUR.

PUR – Polyurethane, invented in 1937 by researchers working with Otto Bayer, has been manufactured industrially since the 1950s. Depending on the raw materials, polyurethanes are either hard and brittle or soft and elastic. This material can also be foamed up. Applications: Soft foam materials for mattresses and car seats, rigid foams as construction materials, thermoplastic elastomers for sporting equipment.

PUR – Polyurethan, *1937 von Forschern um Otto Bayer entwickelt, wird seit den 1950er Jahren industriell gefertigt. Je nach Ausgangsstoff sind die Polyurethane hart und spröde oder weich und elastisch. Zusätzlich kann der Werkstoff aufgeschäumt werden. Anwendungen: Weichschaumstoffe für Matratzen oder Autositze; Hartschäume als Konstruktionsmaterial; thermoplastische Elastomere für Sportartikel.*

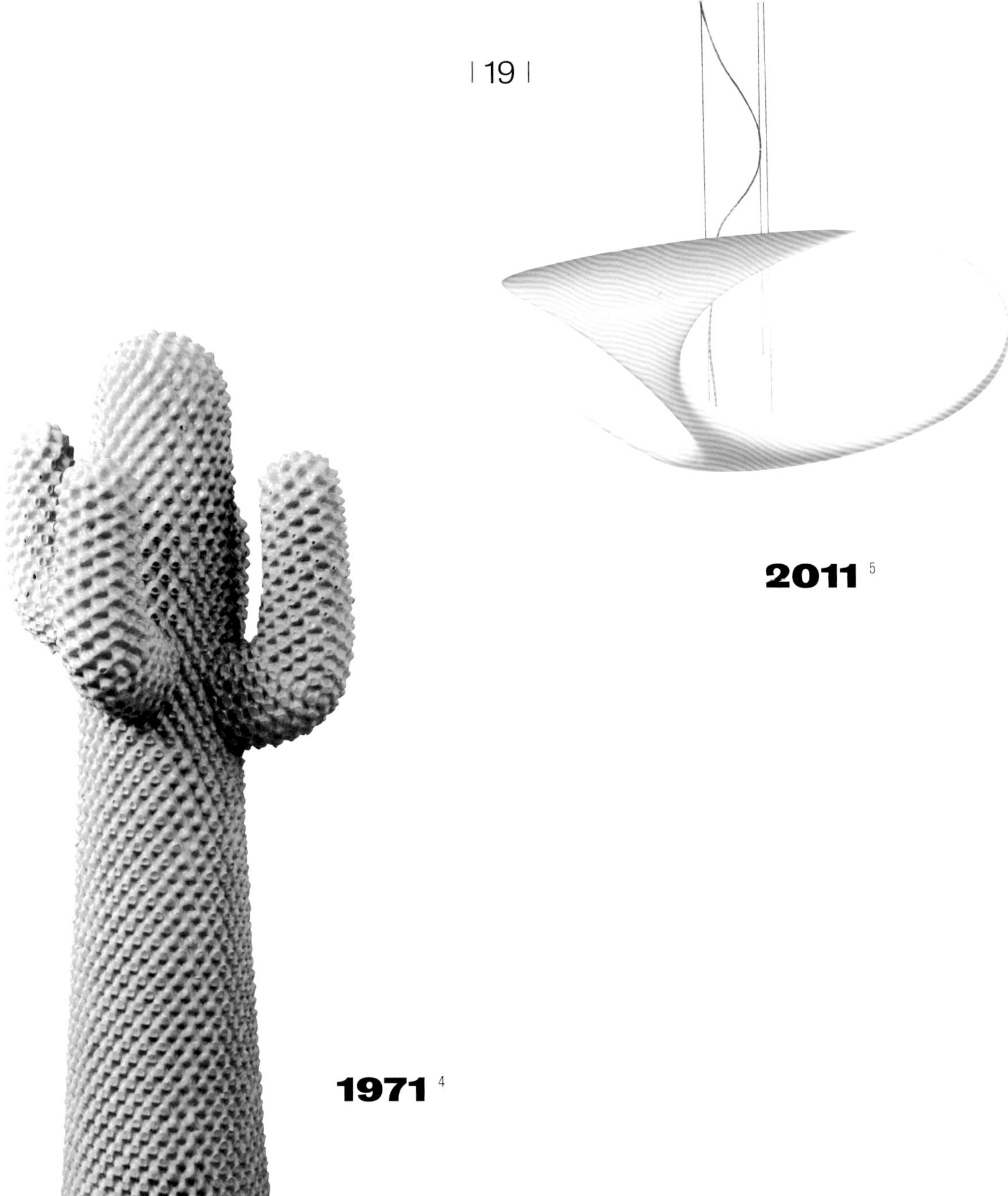

2011 [5]

1971 [4]

1. **1958 Egg™,** Fritz Hansen, Denmark, Design: Arne Jacobsen
2. **1966 Malitte,** Gavina, Italy, Design: Roberto Sebastian Matta
3. **1968 Garden Egg,** Elastogran, Germany, Design: Peter Ghyczy
4. **1971 Cactus,** Gufram, Italy, Design: Guido Drocco, Franco Mello
5. **2011 Clover,** Kundalini, Italy, Design: Brodie Neill

2000 [3]

1998 [2]

1966 [1]

PC.

PC – Polycarbonate was developed by the chemist Hermann Schnell in 1953 as an industrially relevant variant based on Bisphenol A. Polycarbonates stand out among the thermoplastics thanks to their high impact strength, stiffness, and heat resistance. Applications: CDs, DVDs, Blu-ray discs, spectacle lenses and visors, suitcases, and glazing. Famous brands: Makrolon and Lexan.

PC – Polycarbonat *wurde 1953 von Chemiker Hermann Schnell als industriell relevante Variante basierend auf Bisphenol A entwickelt. Als thermoplastische Kunststoffe zeichnen sich Polycarbonate durch eine hohe Schlagzähigkeit, Steifigkeit und Hitzebeständigkeit aus. Anwendungen: CD, DVD, Blu-ray Disc, Brillengläser und Visiere, Koffer, Verglasungen. Bekannte Marken: Makrolon und Lexan.*

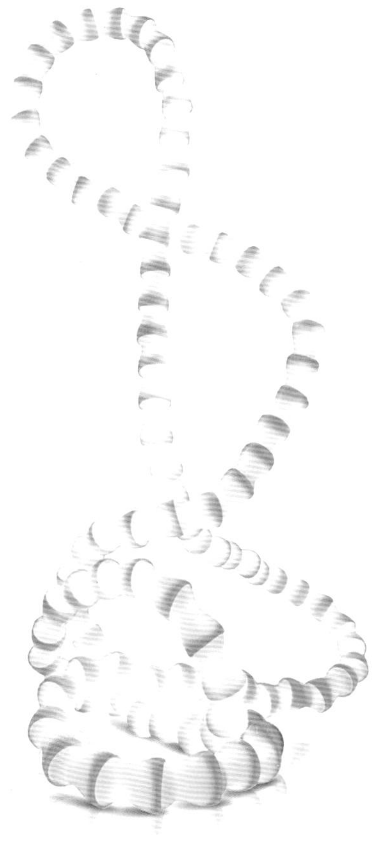

2006 4

2016 5

1. **1966 Lamy 2000,** Lamy, Germany, Design: Gerd Alfred Müller
2. **1998 iMac,** Apple, USA, Design: Jonathan Ive
3. **2000 Rimowa Salsa,** Rimowa, Germany, Design: In-house Design
4. **2006 Abyss,** Kundalini, Italy, Design: Osko+Deichmann
5. **2016 Printable Eco Bottle,** Tupperware, Belgium, Design: Tupperware Worldwide Product Development Team

UP.

UP – Unsaturated polyester can be hardened – most commonly in combination with styrene – to create a duroplastic which is frequently used for larger, glass-fiber-reinforced injection molded parts in design applications. By contrast, saturated polyester is the raw material for thermoplastics such as PET, which is used to make drinks bottles and textiles. Famous trademarks: Dacron, Trevira, and Vestan.

UP – Aus ungesättigtem Polyester *lässt sich, meist in Kombination mit Styrol, durch Härtung ein duroplastischer Kunststoff herstellen, der im Design häufig glasfaserverstärkt für größere Spritzgussteile verwendet wird. Dagegen ist gesättigter Polyester der Ausgangsstoff für thermoplastische Kunststoffe wie beispielsweise PET, die für Getränkeflaschen oder Textilien verwendet werden. Bekannte Handelsnamen: Dacron, Trevira und Vestan.*

1967 [4]

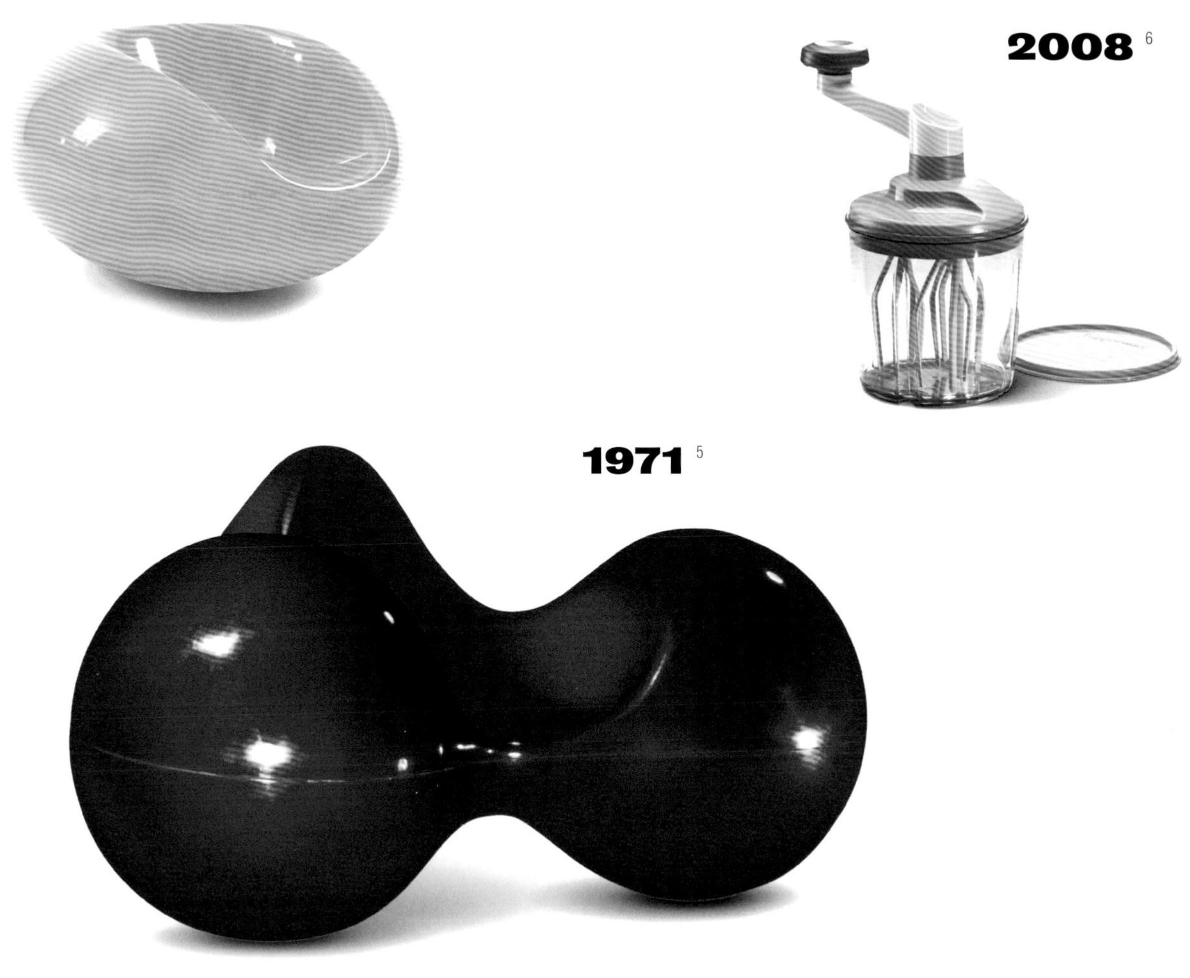

2008 [6]

1971 [5]

1. **1948 La Chaise,** Vitra, Switzerland, Design: Charles Eames, Ray Eames
2. **1956 No. 151/Tulip Chair,** Knoll International, USA, Design: Eero Saarinen
3. **1964 BA 1171/Bofinger Chair,** Menzolit-Werke Albert Schmidt for Wilhelm Bofinger, Germany, Design: Helmut Bätzner
4. **1967 Pastilli,** Design: Eero Aarnio, Eero Aarnio Archives, Finland
5. **1971 Tomato,** Design: Eero Aarnio, Eero Aarnio Archives, Finland
6. **2008 T.S. Speedy Chef,** Tupperware, Belgium, Design: Tupperware Worldwide Product Development Team

1970 [3]

1964 [1]

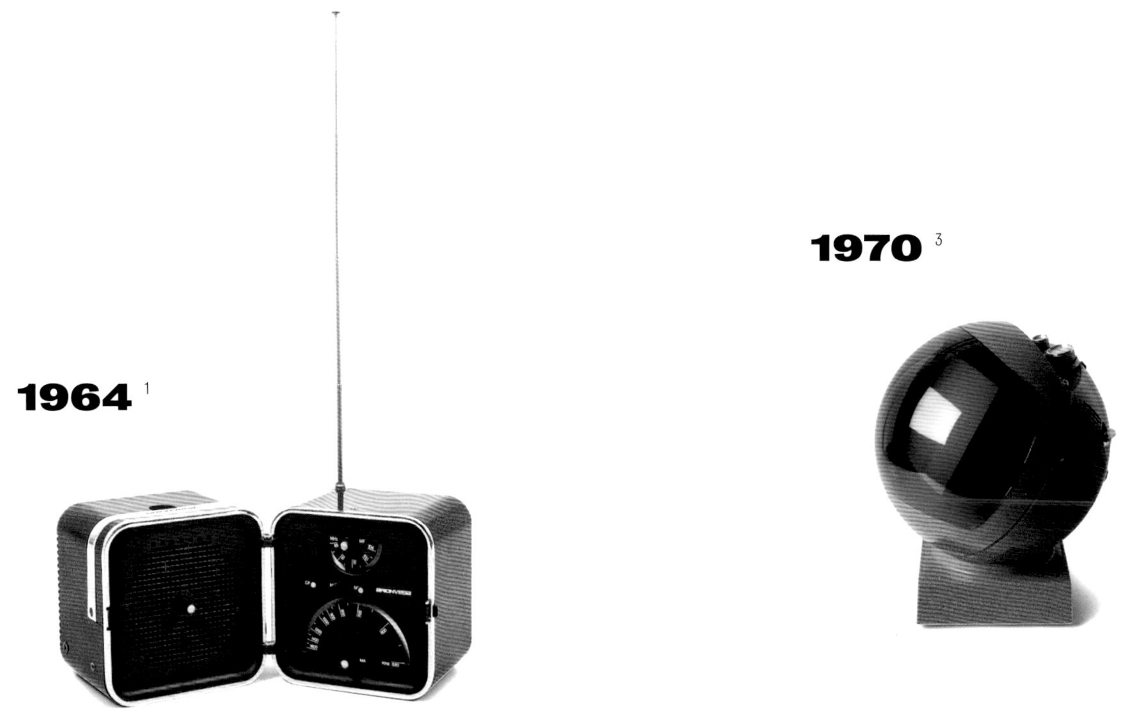

1969 [2]

ABS.

ABS – Acrylonitrile butadiene styrene plastics have been manufactured industrially since the 1950s and are thermoplastics whose chemical composition puts them into the group of highly impact-resistant copolymers. Applications: domestic, consumer and leisure goods, vehicle interiors, housings for electrical appliances, films and pipes in the construction industry.

ABS - Acrylnitril-Butadien-Styrol-*Kunststoffe, seit den 1950er Jahren industriell hergestellt, sind Thermoplaste, die aufgrund ihrer chemischen Zusammensetzung zu den hochschlagfesten Copolymerisaten gehören. Anwendungen: Haushalts-, Konsum- und Freizeitprodukte, Interieur von Fahrzeugen, Gehäuse von Elektrogeräten, Folien und Rohre in der Bauindustrie.*

1. **1964 Radio Cube TS 502,** Brionvega, Italy, Design: Marco Zanuso, Richard Sapper
2. **1969 Toot-a-Loop, Panasonic Radio Model R-72,** Matsushita Electric Industrial, Japan, Design: unknown
3. **1970 Nivico TV, Model 3240 GM,** JVC, Japan, Design: unknown
4. **1970 Weltron 2005,** Weltron, Japan, Design: unknown
5. **2009 Air Multiplier™,** Dyson, UK, Design: James Dyson
6. **2014 Drop,** Fritz Hansen, Denmark, Design: Arne Jacobsen, 1958

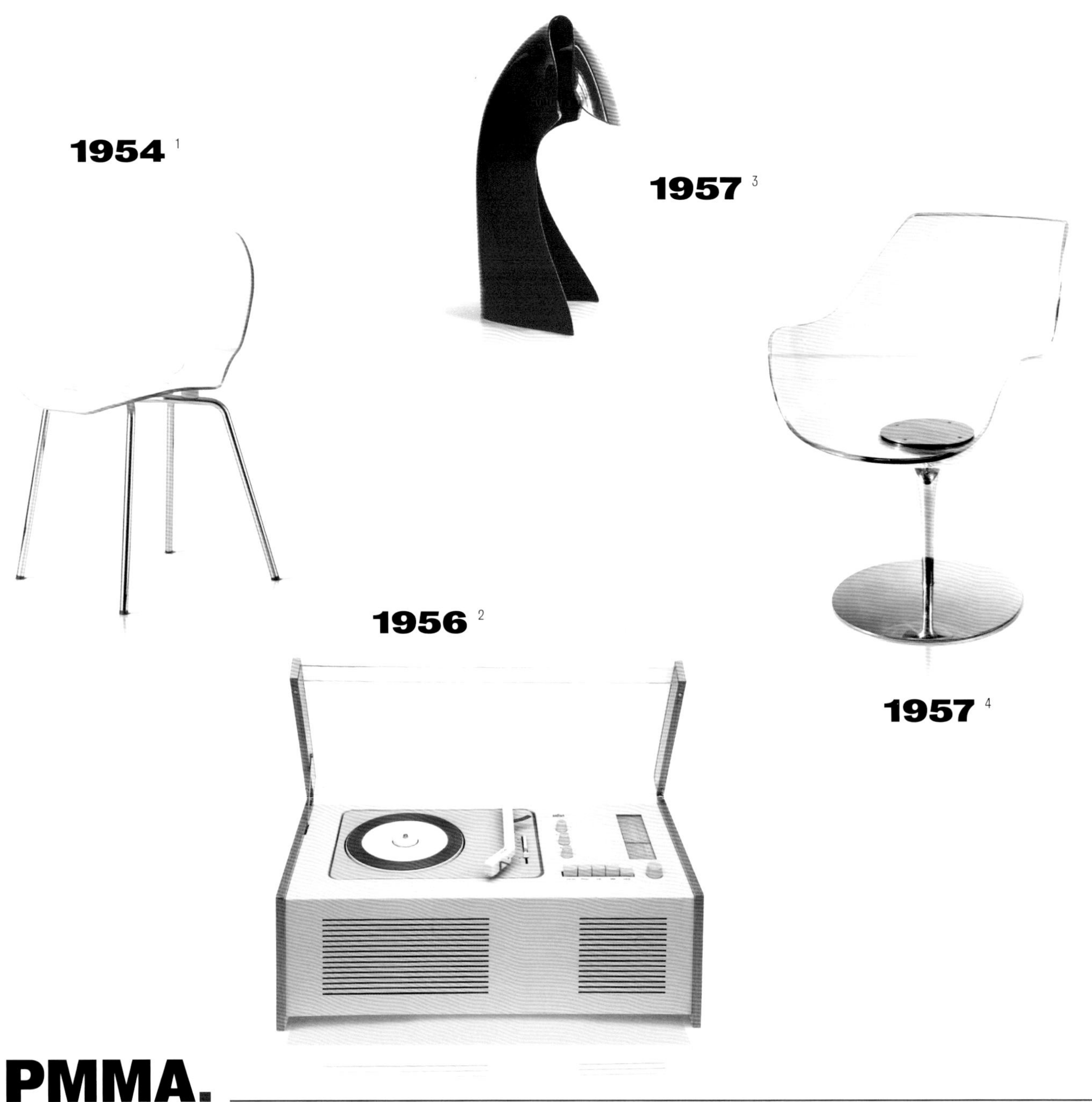

PMMA.

PMMA – Polymethyl methacrylate, invented in Darmstadt, Germany, in 1933 by chemists working with Dr. Otto Röhm, is made via the radical polymerization of methyl methacrylate. PMMA has a very high light transmission and weather resistance. It also offers the greatest surface hardness of all thermoplastics. It is used in automobiles, luminaires, optical and communication applications, construction, and architecture. The most famous brand is PLEXIGLAS®.

PMMA – Polymethylmethacrylat, *1933 von Chemikern rund um Dr. Otto Röhm in Darmstadt erfunden, wird durch radikalische Polymerisation aus Methylmethacrylat hergestellt. PMMA hat eine sehr hohe Transmission und Witterungsbeständigkeit sowie die höchste Oberflächenhärte aller thermoplastischen Kunststoffe. Anwendung in Automobilen, Leuchten, Optik und Kommunikation, Bau und Architektur. Die bekannteste Marke ist PLEXIGLAS®.*

1968 [6]

1991 [8]

1967 [5]

1969 [7]

1. **1954 VB 101 w/PLEXIGLAS® Chair,** Vitra, Switzerland, Design: Hans Theodor Baumann, 1952/53
2. **1956 Radio-Phono-Combination SK 4,** Photo: Braun SK 6/SK 61, Braun, Germany, Design: Hans Gugelot, Dieter Rams
3. **1957 Table Lamp,** Heinz Hecht for HL Leuchten, Germany, Design: Hanns Hoffmann-Lederer
4. **1957 Champagne,** Formes Nouvelles, France, Design: Estelle Laverne, Erwine Laverne
5. **1967 Gherpe,** Poltronova, Italy, Design: Superstudio
6. **1968 Bubble Chair,** Design: Eero Aarnio, Eero Aarnio Archives, Finland
7. **1969 Black ST 201,** Brionvega, Italy, Design: Marco Zanuso, Richard Sapper
8. **1991 Basic,** Alfi, Germany, Design: Ross Lovegrove, Julian Brown

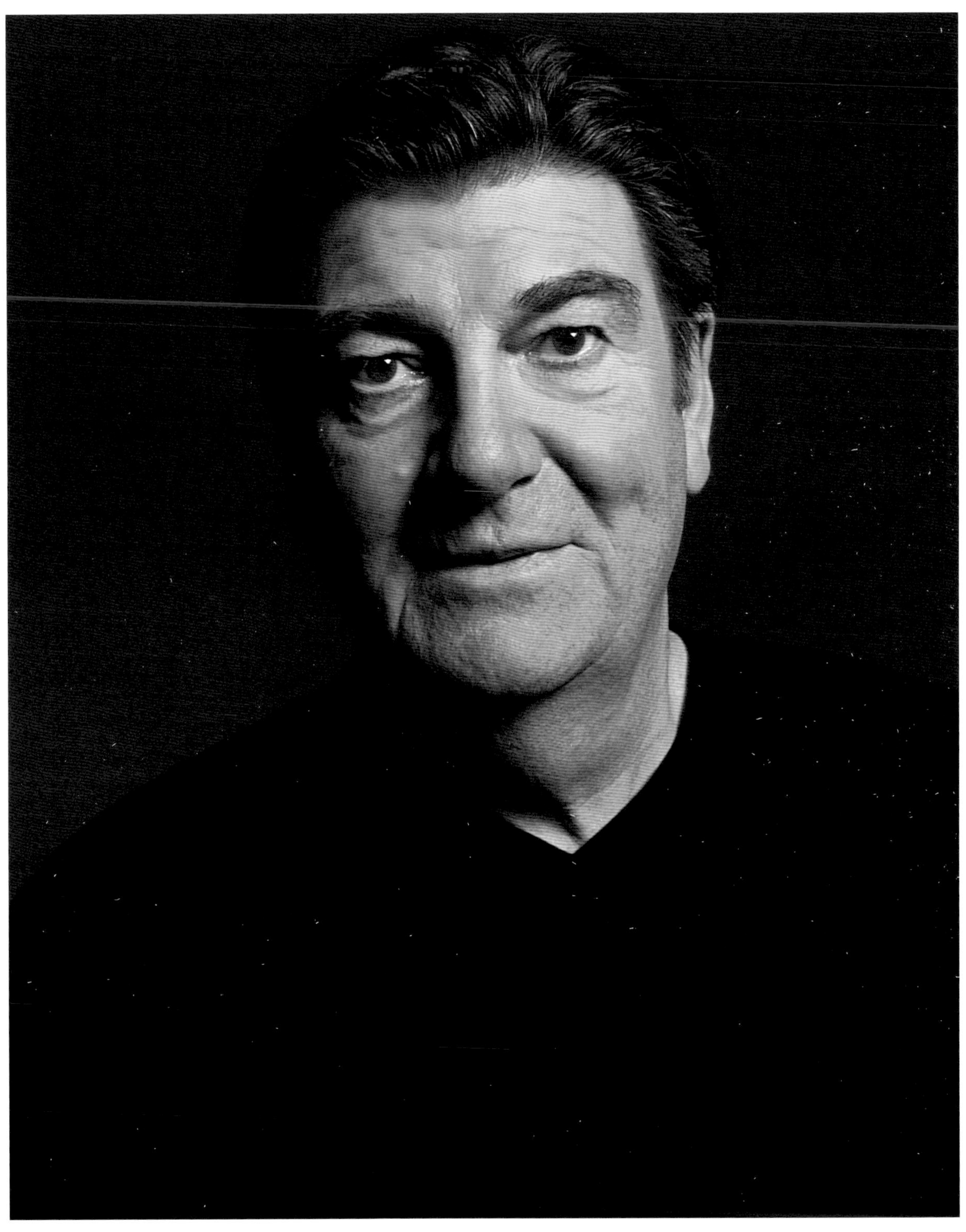

Material and design. On the aesthetics of plastic

Interview with Prof. Dr. Peter Zec, founder and CEO of Red Dot

From the very beginning, the history of design has been linked to the history of technology and the materials available. In the 19th century, people were introduced not only to industrially manufactured products but also to chemically produced materials. The development of synthetic materials has led to many debates in design and architecture, particularly since the beginning of modernism. Discussions centered on technical and aesthetic functions of forms and materials.

Prof. Dr. Peter Zec, founder and CEO of Red Dot, encounters innovative products and materials every year as part of the Red Dot Design Award. The results of the competition are published annually in the Red Dot Design Yearbooks. In this interview with the editorial team, he talks about the significance of plastic materials in design and architecture and the question of what tomorrow's world could look like.

Professor Zec, in 2017 you dedicated an exhibition to the material and the brand that is PLEXIGLAS®. Why did you give the exhibition the title "From an inspiring material to innovative design"?

Designers, architects and companies have fallen into the trap of believing that only new materials can result in modern and innovative design. But even the very best selection of the newest materials will not automatically create a good and useful form for users. PLEXIGLAS® is a material invented back in 1933 by Dr. Otto Röhm and his staff. It has been inspiring designers and architects to create innovative forms ever since.

Can you give some examples of design and architecture that have been inspired by the PLEXIGLAS® material?

In terms of design, the first object that springs to mind is the Phonosuper SK 4 designed by Hans Gugelot and Dieter Rams for Braun AG. It was nicknamed "Snow White's coffin" because of the device's see-through lid. The combination of radio and record player with the transparent cover heralded a new era in the design of electrical devices in the 1950s, because the product was ground-breaking for an entire industry and for the design of electrical devices in terms of its clarity and user friendliness. As far as architecture is concerned, one undisputed milestone is the tent canopy construction of Munich's Olympic Stadium designed by Günter Behnisch and inspired by the designs and form studies of architect Frei Otto, which won the Pritzker Architecture Prize soon after his death in 2015.

Do we even still notice the material once it has been transformed into an object? Or do we just see the object and no longer see the material?

Design objects are items intended for use. The better they are designed, the more naturally they perform their function. They seem to merge into their day-to-day use. At that moment, we only see what we use the objects for. And yet there is always also a moment when we notice its material manifestation.

After all, we hold lots of objects in our hands every day. This non-verbal communication is shaped in particular by the material. It influences not only the function but also the aesthetic of the product.

How can this impact of materials be used for design and also for communication?

The Red Dot Design Award is a fine example of companies repeatedly using certain materials in a targeted way to inform the aesthetic of their products and their brand. Just think of Apple, Kartell or Dyson. The continuity in the language of form and material aesthetic shapes the brand as a whole. In this way, materials are not only part of a successful brand and corporate history – they are also an expression of our design and lifestyle culture.

Is every material a product of a certain era? Does every material have its day?

If a material can shape the aesthetic of a brand, then of course it can also shape a certain period in design or architecture. Let's not forget that entire periods in the history of humans are named after the materials predominantly used during those specific eras.

Plastic materials have been part of our lives since the era of industrialization; they are an expression of modernity. PLEXIGLAS® has also been part of our lives for decades now. The material was originally used primarily in its clear form, but precisely this transparency and lack of color was soon used to render colors exactly, either colored or later also illuminated with color. The material seems ageless, because it reinvents itself over time. The author Roland Barthes pointed out back in the 1950s that plastic was more than a substance and embodied the very idea of infinite transformation. This makes it a timeless material and a constant source of inspiration for designers and architects.

Does that mean that the material itself already constitutes design?

The material alone does not make the design. Technical objects have to be formed and organized. Answering the question of how to combine one part with another or one material with another to create a structure and a usable form is key to understanding design and architecture.

Materials and ideas appear to have a mutual influence. Is the design process always triggered by an idea, or can it be the material that forms the basis for the design process?

Both of these scenarios are possible. Time after time in the Red Dot Award: Product Design, we see innovative materials in search of a design idea and application. By contrast, in the Red Dot Award: Design Concept we observe innovative concepts looking for the right material. But the choice of material shouldn't be left to chance; it needs to be a conscious decision. That's because nowadays access to plastic materials is almost always linked to technology, expertise and production methods like all of the thermoplastic methods – for example injection molding or extrusion. And this path should lead designers and architects to competent partners and industrial firms. Consequently, they need to seek dialog with materials manufacturers.

Do products made from plastic play a more significant role in design now than 25 or 50 years ago?

Even in the first design competition back in 1955, some of the winning products were encased predominantly in plastic. The 1960s and 1970s in particular then saw the emergence of design icons that have long since become classic pieces and that would be unthinkable without plastic. Just think of the Panton Chair or the Bofinger Chair, both of which stand out thanks to their monolithic shape. Or what about the radios and TVs from Brionvega, which were designed by Marco Zanuso and Richard Sapper? In the 1980s, the Sony Walkman and the Swatch watch rose to cult status. At the end of the 1990s it was the Apple iMac, while at the start of the noughties it was the Apple iPod. By the end of that decade, the household appliances from Dyson had taken the world by storm. Quite often these products changed entire industries. And the possibilities for use are increasing as the properties of plastic materials become more and more diverse.

Are plastic materials becoming increasingly important for designers and architects?

The significance of plastic materials is constantly on the rise, especially the significance of premium plastic materials. They are becoming more resilient and robust and can be formed into virtually any shape. As far as PLEXIGLAS® is concerned, more than anything else it's the touch and feel of the product that makes it stand out. This makes the material interesting for lots of different industries, in particular for luminaires and lighting applications, for household and kitchen appliances and for medical devices and diagnostics, but also for the automotive sector, where tailored materials offer lightweight construction solutions and influence both the vehicle interior and exterior. Extremely thin yet supple plastic films are also used in smartphone and smartwatch displays as well as high-resolution screens.

Do you think that the development of plastic materials will someday come to an end? In other words, how can we imagine the development of plastic materials and the world we will inhabit in the future?

In principle, human history and human artefacts reflect a process that journeys from the natural to the artificial. Although humans are biological beings, the world we live in now and the world we will inhabit in the future is an artificially created world. The natural and the artificial are intersecting or merging. We only have to think of the example of prosthetics to be reminded of numerous examples of products in the history of design and of the Red Dot Design Award that constantly push, transcend or break down the boundaries between the natural and the artificial. Plastic materials are an expression and part of this development, because they provide the foundations for how we will live tomorrow. Driverless cars, robotics, virtual reality and artificial intelligence are more than just buzzwords. The applications that we are already seeing and experiencing in design today are showing us that many industries and sectors are in transition and we are under way to the next phase in our society.

Many thanks for speaking with us.

Material und Design. Zur Ästhetik des Kunststoffs

Interview mit Prof. Dr. Peter Zec, Initiator und CEO von Red Dot

Die Geschichte des Designs ist von Anfang an mit der Geschichte der Technik und den verfügbaren Werkstoffen verknüpft. Im 19. Jahrhundert lernen die Menschen nicht nur industriell gefertigte Produkte kennen, sondern auch Materialien, die auf chemischem Wege hergestellt werden. Die Entwicklung synthetischer Materialien hat insbesondere seit Beginn der Moderne zu vielen Debatten in Design und Architektur geführt. Diskutiert wurde über technische und ästhetische Funktionen von Formen und Materialien.

Prof. Dr. Peter Zec, Initiator und CEO von Red Dot, begegnen jedes Jahr im Red Dot Design Award innovative Produkte und Materialien. Die Ergebnisse des Wettbewerbs werden jährlich in den Red Dot Design Yearbooks veröffentlicht. Im Interview mit der Redaktion nimmt er Stellung zur Bedeutung von Kunststoffen in Design und Architektur und geht auf die Frage ein, wie die Welt von morgen aussehen könnte.

Herr Professor Zec, im Jahr 2017 haben Sie dem Werkstoff und der Marke PLEXIGLAS® eine Ausstellung gewidmet. Warum haben Sie der Ausstellung den Titel „Vom inspirierenden Material zum innovativen Design" gegeben?

Designer, Architekten und Unternehmen sitzen bisweilen dem Missverständnis auf, dass nur neue Materialien modernes und innovatives Design hervorbringen. Aber die schönste Auswahl der neuesten Materialien bringt nicht automatisch eine gute und nützliche Form für den Anwender hervor. PLEXIGLAS® ist ein Werkstoff, der bereits 1933 von Dr. Otto Röhm und seinen Mitarbeitern erfunden wurde. Seither hat er immer wieder Designer und Architekten zu innovativen Formen inspiriert.

Könnten Sie Beispiele nennen, bei denen Design und Architektur durch den Werkstoff PLEXIGLAS® inspiriert worden sind?

Im Design denke ich vor allem an den von Hans Gugelot und Dieter Rams für die Braun AG entworfenen „Schneewittchensarg": Phonosuper SK 4. Der Ausdruck verdankt sich der transparenten Abdeckung des Gerätes. Die Kombination aus Radio und Plattenspieler mit dem transparenten Deckel läutete in den 1950er Jahren eine neue Epoche im Elektrogerätedesign ein, weil das Produkt in seiner Klarheit und Benutzerfreundlichkeit für eine ganze Branche und die Gestaltung von Elektrogeräten beispielgebend war. Ein Meilenstein in der Architektur ist ohne Zweifel die von Günter Behnisch entworfene Zeltdachkonstruktion des Olympiastadions in München, die von den Entwürfen und den Formstudien des Architekten Frei Otto inspiriert war, der kurz nach seinem Tod im Jahr 2015 den Pritzker-Preis für Architektur erhalten hat.

Nimmt man das Material denn überhaupt noch wahr, wenn es sich erst einmal in ein Objekt verwandelt hat? Oder sieht man nur noch den Gegenstand und nicht mehr das Material?

Designobjekte sind Gegenstände, die für den Gebrauch bestimmt sind. Je besser sie gestaltet sind, desto selbstverständlicher erfüllen sie ihre Funktion. Sie scheinen förmlich im täglichen Gebrauch aufzugehen. In diesem Augenblick nehmen wir nur wahr, was wir mit den Dingen tun. Und doch gibt es immer auch den Moment, in dem wir die materielle Erscheinung wahrnehmen. Wir haben ja täglich viele Dinge in der Hand. Diese nonverbale Ebene der Kommunikation wird insbesondere durch das Material bestimmt. Es beeinflusst nicht nur die Funktion, sondern auch die Ästhetik.

Wie lässt sich diese Wirkung von Materialien für das Design und auch für die Kommunikation nutzen?

Im Red Dot Design Award lässt sich sehr schön beobachten, wie Unternehmen immer wieder bestimmte Materialien gezielt einsetzen, um die Ästhetik ihrer Produkte und ihrer Marke zu prägen. Denken Sie beispielsweise an Apple, Kartell oder Dyson. Die Kontinuität in der Formensprache und Materialästhetik wirkt markenprägend. Auf diese Weise sind Materialien nicht nur Teil einer erfolgreichen Marken- und Unternehmensgeschichte – sie sind auch Ausdruck unserer Design- und Lebenskultur.

Ist jedes Material an eine bestimmte Zeit gebunden? Hat jedes Material seine Zeit?

Wenn ein Material die Ästhetik einer Marke prägen kann, dann kann es natürlich auch eine bestimmte Zeit im Design oder in der Architektur prägen. Vergessen wir nicht, dass ganze Perioden in der Geschichte der Menschheit nach Materialien benannt wurden, die in einer bestimmten Zeit vorherrschend waren.

Kunststoffe begleiten uns seit der Industrialisierung und sind Ausdruck der Moderne. Auch PLEXIGLAS® begleitet uns seit Jahrzehnten. Wurde das Material ursprünglich vor allem in seiner glasklaren Urform verwendet, ist es gerade diese Transparenz und Farblosigkeit, die schon bald dazu genutzt wurde, Farben exakt wiederzugeben, ob nun eingefärbt oder später auch farbig beleuchtet. Das Material scheint nicht zu altern, weil es sich immer wieder neu erfindet. Der Schriftsteller Roland Barthes hat bereits in den 1950er Jahren darauf hingewiesen, dass Kunststoff nicht nur eine Substanz ist, sondern die Idee einer unendlichen Verwandlung verkörpert. Das macht es zu einem zeitlosen Material und zu einer beständigen Inspirationsquelle für Designer und Architekten.

Ist Material denn bereits Design?

Allein das Material macht noch nicht das Design aus. Technische Gegenstände müssen geformt und organisiert werden. Die Frage, wie sich ein Teil mit dem anderen oder ein Werkstoff mit dem anderen zu einer Struktur und einer gebrauchsfertigen Form verbindet, ist ein Schlüssel zum Verständnis von Design und Architektur.

Materialien und Ideen scheinen sich gegenseitig zu beeinflussen. Steht am Anfang des Designprozesses immer eine Idee oder bildet das Material den Ausgangspunkt für den Gestaltungsprozess?

Beides lässt sich beobachten. Im Red Dot Award: Product Design sehen wir immer wieder innovative Materialien, die förmlich nach einer gestalterischen Idee und einer Anwendung suchen. Im Red Dot Award: Design Concept sehen wir dagegen innovative Konzepte, die nach dem passenden Material suchen. Die Wahl des Materials sollte aber nicht dem Zufall überlassen werden, sondern eine bewusste Entscheidung sein. Denn der Zugang zu Kunststoffen ist heute fast immer mit Technologie, Know-how und Fertigungsverfahren wie alle thermoplastischen Methoden – zum Beispiel Spritzgießen oder Extrudieren – verbunden. Und dieser Weg sollte für Designer und Architekten zu kompetenten Partnern und Industrie-

unternehmen führen. Sie sollten daher den Dialog mit Materialherstellern suchen.

Haben Produkte aus Kunststoff heute einen höheren Stellenwert im Design als vor 25 oder 50 Jahren?

Bereits im ersten Designwettbewerb von 1955 wurden Produkte ausgezeichnet, deren Gehäuse im Wesentlichen aus Kunststoff bestand. Insbesondere die 1960er und 1970er Jahre haben dann Designikonen hervorgebracht, die längst zu Klassikern geworden sind und ohne Kunststoff nicht denkbar gewesen wären. Denken Sie nur an den Panton Chair oder den Bofinger-Stuhl, die beide durch ihre monolithische Form bestechen. Oder nehmen Sie die Radios und Fernseher von Brionvega, die von Marco Zanuso und Richard Sapper gestaltet wurden. In den 1980er Jahren haben der Sony Walkman und die Swatch-Uhr Kultstatus erreicht. Ende der 1990er Jahre war es der Apple iMac, Anfang der 2000er Jahre der Apple iPod. Zum Ende der Dekade die Haushaltsgeräte von Dyson. Nicht selten haben diese Produkte ganze Branchen verändert. Und da die Eigenschaften von Kunststoffen immer vielfältiger werden, erweitern sich auch die Anwendungsmöglichkeiten.

Werden Kunststoffe immer wichtiger für Designer und Architekten?

Die Bedeutung der Kunststoffe nimmt kontinuierlich zu, insbesondere die Bedeutung hochwertiger Kunststoffe. Sie werden widerstandsfähiger und belastbarer und lassen sich nahezu beliebig formen. Mit Blick auf PLEXIGLAS® sind insbesondere die haptischen und optischen Eigenschaften herausragend. Das macht den Werkstoff für viele Branchen interessant, insbesondere für die Licht- und Leuchtenanwendungen, für Haushalts- und Küchengeräte sowie die Medizintechnik, aber auch im Automobilbereich, wo maßgeschneiderte Werkstoffe Lösungen zur Leichtbaukonstruktion liefern und das Exterieur wie Interieur von Fahrzeugen beeinflussen. Extrem dünne und zugleich biegsame Kunststofffolien finden wir zudem bei Displays von Smartphones und Smartwatches sowie hochauflösenden Bildschirmen.

Glauben Sie, dass die Entwicklung neuer Kunststoffe irgendwann an ein Ende gelangt? Anders gefragt: Wie kann man sich die Entwicklung der Kunststoffe und die Welt, in der wir künftig leben, vorstellen?

Die Geschichte des Menschen und seiner Artefakte liest sich im Grunde wie ein Prozess, der sich von der Natürlichkeit zur Künstlichkeit bewegt. Auch wenn der Mensch ein biologisches Wesen ist, so ist die Welt, in der er heute und in Zukunft lebt, eine künstlich geschaffene Welt. Natürlichkeit und Künstlichkeit überlagern sich oder verschmelzen miteinander. Denken Sie nur an den Bereich der Prothetik. Hierzu finden sich in der Geschichte des Designs und im Red Dot Design Award zahlreiche Beispiele von Produkten, die die Grenze von Natürlichkeit und Künstlichkeit immer weiter verschieben, überschreiten oder aufheben. Kunststoffe sind Ausdruck und Teil dieser Entwicklung, denn sie schaffen die Grundlagen dafür, wie wir morgen leben werden. Autonomes Fahren, Robotik, virtuelle Realität oder künstliche Intelligenz sind mehr als nur Schlagworte. Die Anwendungen, die wir bereits heute im Design sehen und erleben, signalisieren uns, dass viele Branchen und Industriezweige im Umbruch und wir auf dem Weg in die nächste Gesellschaft sind.

Herzlichen Dank für das Gespräch!

FORM FOLLOWS EXPERIENCE

PLEXIGLAS® COMBINES THE TRADITIONAL WITH THE MODERN

Plastics are the materials of the modern world. The scientific foundation for an understanding of this new, modern class of materials was laid in 1920 by chemist Hermann Staudinger in an article on polymerization. He later went on to receive the Nobel prize for his work.

The 1930s marked the start of one of the most significant decades for the plastics industry. Many of the synthetic materials that are widely used today were invented in that period. Take for example the hard, transparent sheets of polymethyl methacrylate, invented by Dr Otto Röhm and his team at Röhm & Haas in Darmstadt, Germany in 1933. The new material was registered as a trademark that same year and was given the name PLEXIGLAS®.

Shortly after, the researchers developed PLEXIGLAS® molding compounds for use in injection molding processes, thereby revolutionizing the processing of plastics. For the first time, it was possible to produce large numbers of precisely molded components in a single process step and to do so cost effectively.

PLEXIGLAS® components have since had an impact on countless industries. In the automotive industry, the material has had a firm place in the production of taillight covers since the mid-1950s. It has helped turn the originally small, functional signaling lights with a glass cover into the large, brand-specific design elements that we know today. This is just one of the many ways in which creative minds have used the benefits offered by PLEXIGLAS® to make their ideas become reality.

PLEXIGLAS® VERBINDET TRADITION MIT MODERNE

Kunststoffe sind das Material der Moderne. Den wissenschaftlichen Grundstein für das Verständnis dieser neuen, modernen Werkstoffklasse legt im Jahr 1920 der Chemiker Hermann Staudinger mit seinem Artikel über die Polymerisation. Für seine Arbeiten wird Staudinger später den Nobelpreis erhalten.

Mit den 1930er Jahren bricht eines der wichtigsten Jahrzehnte der Kunststoffindustrie an. Innerhalb einer Dekade werden viele der heute weit verbreiteten synthetischen Materialien erfunden. Im Jahr 1933 zum Beispiel harte, transparente Platten aus Polymethylmethacrylat – entdeckt von Chemikern rund um Dr. Otto Röhm bei Röhm & Haas in Darmstadt. Das neue Material wurde noch im selben Jahr als Marke angemeldet und erhielt den Namen PLEXIGLAS®.

Schon bald darauf entwickelten die Forscher PLEXIGLAS® Formmassen zur Anwendung im Spritzgießverfahren und revolutionierten damit die Kunststoffverarbeitung: Erstmals waren hohe Stückzahlen sowie eine kostengünstige Produktion von präzisen Formteilen in nur einem Arbeitsschritt möglich.

Bauteile aus PLEXIGLAS® haben seitdem zahlreiche Branchen verändert. In der Automobilindustrie hat der Werkstoff seit Mitte der 1950er Jahre seinen festen Platz bei der Herstellung von Abdeckungen für Heckleuchten. Er hat dazu beigetragen, dass sich die ursprünglich kleinen, funktionalen Signalleuchten mit einer Abdeckung aus Glas inzwischen zu großflächigen, markenspezifischen Gestaltungselementen entwickelt haben. Nur ein Beispiel von vielen, wie kreative Köpfe seit Jahrzehnten die Möglichkeiten von PLEXIGLAS® nutzen, um ihre Ideen in die Tat umzusetzen.

1957

Material aesthetics. In the 1950s, designer and artist Hanns Hoffmann-Lederer designs luminaires from PLEXIGLAS® by forming the material into waves or sheaths and adding a light bulb.

Materialästhetik. *Der Designer und Künstler Hanns Hoffmann-Lederer entwirft in den 1950er Jahren Leuchten aus PLEXIGLAS®, indem er das Material zu Wellen oder Hüllen formt und mit einer Glühlampe versieht.*

Design: *Hanns Hoffmann-Lederer*

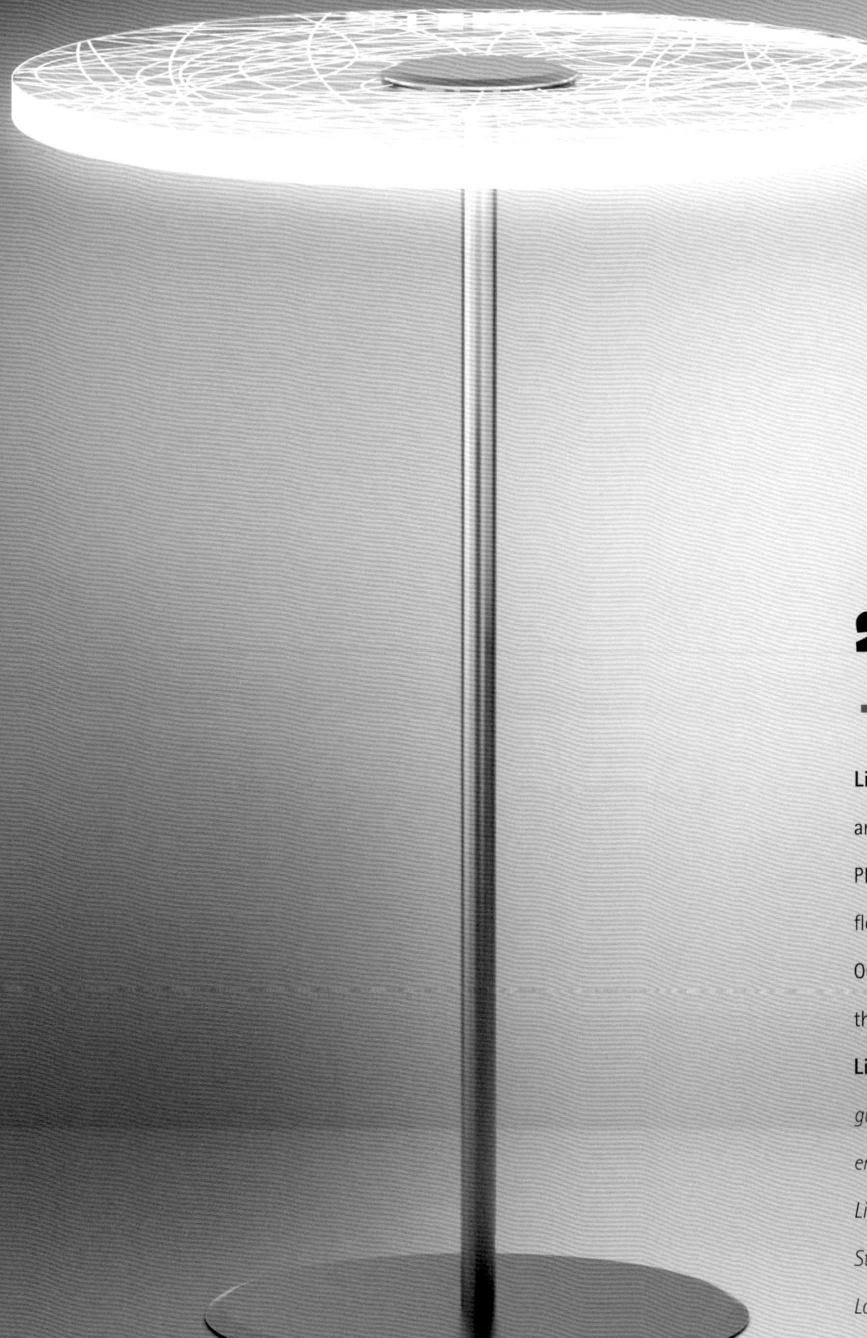

2017

Light aesthetics. LEDs, laser technology and the high light guiding properties of PLEXIGLAS® create a graphical game of floating lines. The light intensity of the OCARI® Stelaro luminaire is controlled by the depth and width of the laser engraving.
Lichtästhetik. *LEDs, Lasertechnik und die guten Lichtleiteigenschaften von PLEXIGLAS® erzeugen ein grafisches Spiel schwebender Linien. Die Lichtstärke der OCARI®-Leuchte Stelaro wird über die Tiefe und Breite der Lasergravur gesteuert.*
Design: *Ingmar Boos, Daniel Schulz*

2000

Premium brand. The exterior of the relaunched MINI retains the features of the cult car, but sets standards with new technology. The innovative A-pillar covers made from PLEXIGLAS® in Piano Black underscore the MINI's premium quality and the larger windscreen.

Premiummarke. *Mit dem Relaunch des MINI behält das Exterieur die Charakteristik des Kultautos, setzt aber mit neuer Technik Maßstäbe. Dabei unterstreichen die innovativen A-Säulenblenden aus PLEXIGLAS® in Piano Black die Premiumqualität des MINI und seine größere Frontscheibe.*

Design: *BMW Group*

1959

Cult car. When Alec Issigonis sketched his idea for the Mini on a napkin, he created an urban small car for the 'Swinging Sixties': with a transverse engine and central instruments – regardless of whether left-hand or right-hand drive.

Kultauto. *Als Alec Issigonis seine Idee des Mini auf eine Serviette zeichnete, schuf er einen urbanen Kleinwagen für die „Swinging Sixties": mit quer eingebautem Motor und zentralen Instrumenten – unabhängig von Links- oder Rechtslenkung.*

Design: *Alec Issigonis*

1969

Moon landing. The crystal-clear acrylic atmospherically surrounds the aluminum reflectors of the VP Globe lamp. It was materials like PLEXIGLAS® that Verner Panton used in the year of the moon landing to create an iconic design piece with an aesthetic reflective of a belief in technology and the future.

Mondlandung. *Atmosphärisch legt sich das glasklare Acryl um die Aluminiumreflektoren der Leuchte VP Globe. Aus Materialien wie PLEXIGLAS® hat Verner Panton im Jahr der Mondlandung eine Ikone des Designs entworfen, deren Ästhetik den Glauben an Technologie und Zukunft widerspiegelt.*

Design: *Verner Panton*

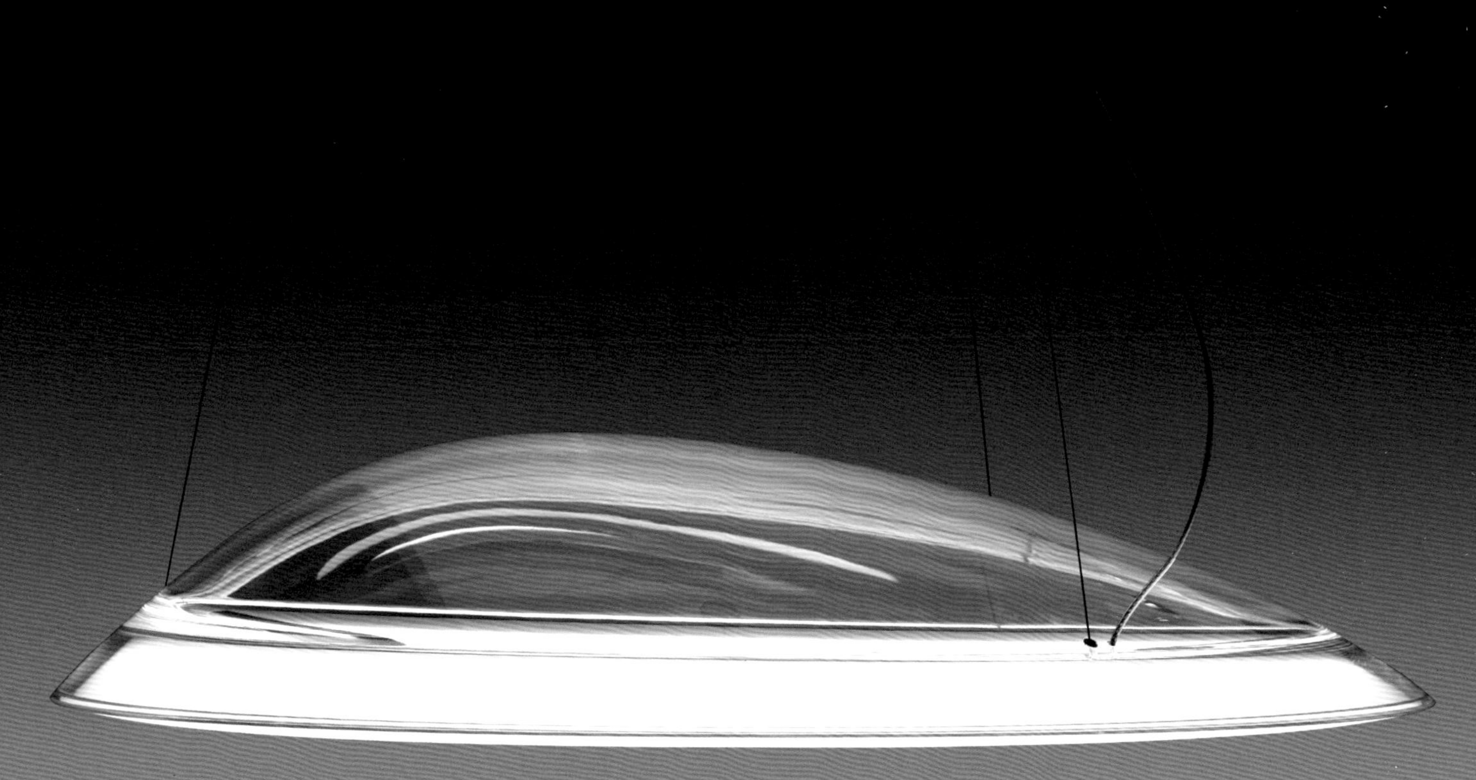

2016

Moon goddess. Pendant luminaire Ameluna combines in its name Artemide's lighting competency and Mercedes-Benz Style's philosophy of sensual clarity with the word 'luna', Italian for 'moon', which is reflected in the transparent luminaire body made from PLEXIGLAS®.

Mondgöttin. *Die Pendelleuchte Ameluna verbindet in ihrem Namen die Lichtkompetenz von Artemide und die Philosophie der sinnlichen Klarheit von Mercedes-Benz Style mit dem Wort Luna, italienisch für Mond, der im transparenten Leuchtenkörper aus PLEXIGLAS® zum Ausdruck kommt.*

Design: *Artemide & Mercedes-Benz Style*

1950

Light signal. In the 1950s, plastic becomes no longer a cheap replacement but a design material in its own right. The design potential of acrylic is recognized early on in automobile design, with PMMA taking over the tail light market. A well-known example is the VW Beetle with rear light covers made from PLEXIGLAS®.

Lichtsignal. *In den 1950er Jahren ist Kunststoff nicht mehr günstiger Ersatzstoff, sondern eigenständiger Werkstoff im Design. Im Automobildesign wird das gestalterische Potenzial von Acrylglas früh erkannt: PMMA gewinnt den Heckleuchtenmarkt für sich. Bekanntes Beispiel ist der VW Käfer mit Heckleuchtenabdeckungen aus PLEXIGLAS®.*

Design: *Volkswagen*

2016

Lighting technology. We cannot fail to notice progress. Or fail to see the light. The rear light made from PLEXIGLAS® emanates security and presence. In conjunction with efficient LED lights, this elegant and dynamic design facilitates better visibility.

Lichttechnologie. *Der Fortschritt ist unverkennbar. Das Licht unübersehbar. Die Rückleuchte aus PLEXIGLAS® vermittelt den Eindruck von Sicherheit und Präsenz. In Verbindung mit effizienten LED-Leuchtmitteln ermöglicht die ebenso elegante wie dynamische Gestaltung eine bessere Wahrnehmung.*

Design: *AUDI*

1972

A feat of engineering. Building stadium roofs poses a major challenge. Their enormous breadth calls for lightweight construction. The tent canopy construction of Munich's Olympic Stadium was a sensation in this regard. Thanks to transparent PLEXIGLAS® sheets, the cable mesh construction blended harmoniously into the surroundings, symbolizing a new era of openness.

Konstruktive Höchstleistung. *Dachkonstruktionen von Stadien sind eine Herausforderung. Die großen Spannweiten erfordern eine leichte Konstruktion. Das Zeltdach des Münchner Olympiastadions war in dieser Hinsicht eine Sensation. Dank transparenter PLEXIGLAS® Platten fügte sich die Seilnetzkonstruktion harmonisch in die Landschaft und symbolisierte eine neue Offenheit.*

Architecture | Architektur:

Behnisch & Partner, Frei Otto

2005

An aesthetic feat of light. Where the Olympic Stadium embodied a new openness, the Allianz Arena is reflective of today's event culture. From 2005, diffusor covers in three colours made from extruded PLEXIGLAS® provided a symphony of light for around ten years, transforming the Allianz Arena into a cathedral of the 21st century.

Ästhetische Lichtleistung. *Verkörperte das Olympiastadion eine neue Offenheit, so ist die Allianz Arena Ausdruck der heutigen Eventkultur. Ab dem Jahr 2005 führten dreifarbige Diffusor-Abdeckungen aus extrudiertem PLEXIGLAS® für rund zehn Jahre die Lichtregie und verwandelten die Allianz Arena in eine Kathedrale des 21. Jahrhunderts.*

Architecture | Architektur:
Herzog & de Meuron

FORM FOLLOWS PERFORMANCE

PLEXIGLAS® MAKES THE DIFFERENCE IN DESIGN AND ARCHITECTURE

"More than a substance, plastic is the very idea of infinite transformation." Author Roland Barthes already articulated this concept in "Mythologies" way back in the 1950s. Where other materials reached their limits, plastics opened up new application and design possibilities.

With its versatile properties, PLEXIGLAS® makes a crucial difference to numerous highly specific applications. Here is one example: plastic sheets can be cut to a precise size and be shaped. These cut-to-size sheets can then be assembled in great number to, for instance, create a uniform building façade that is both translucent and delicate in appearance, yet is still hard-wearing – even under the blazing Nigerian sun.

In different cases, other properties of PLEXIGLAS® play a decisive role. The material not only offers very high light transmission, but is completely colorless in its original state. It therefore replicates colors extremely accurately – whether as a tinted component or under colored light. That is what makes taillights, for example, shine in precisely the right signal colors or enables entire building façades to appear in the company's corporate colors. In other applications, the material directs targeted light onto workplaces or street sections, gives surfaces an elegant glow or extended durability.

PLEXIGLAS® MACHT DEN UNTERSCHIED IN DESIGN UND ARCHITEKTUR

„Plastik ist nicht nur eine Substanz, es ist die Idee ihrer unendlichen Transformation." Der Schriftsteller Roland Barthes hat diese Idee in seinen „Mythen des Alltags" bereits in den 1950er Jahren formuliert. Wo andere Materialien an ihre Grenzen stoßen, schafft Kunststoff neue Anwendungs- und Gestaltungsmöglichkeiten.

PLEXIGLAS® macht durch seine vielfältigen Eigenschaften bei zahlreichen hochspezifischen Anwendungen den Unterschied. Ein Beispiel: Platten aus dem Werkstoff lassen sich exakt zuschneiden und umformen. Aus sehr vielen dieser geformten Zuschnitte kann dann beispielsweise eine homogene Gebäudehülle entstehen, die gleichzeitig transluzent und filigran wirkt und dabei robust ist – selbst gegen die gleißende Sonne in Nigeria.

In anderen Fällen spielen weitere Eigenschaften von PLEXIGLAS® eine entscheidende Rolle: So hat das Material nicht nur eine sehr hohe Lichttransmission, sondern es ist in seiner Urform absolut farblos und gibt daher Farben sehr exakt wieder – ob als eingefärbtes oder farbig beleuchtetes Bauteil. Dadurch erstrahlen beispielsweise Heckleuchten sehr exakt in Signalfarben oder ganze Fassaden in der Corporate Color eines Unternehmens. Bei anderen Anwendungen leitet das Material Licht zielgerichtet auf Arbeitsplätze oder Straßenabschnitte, verleiht Oberflächen einen edlen Glanz und eine lange Haltbarkeit.

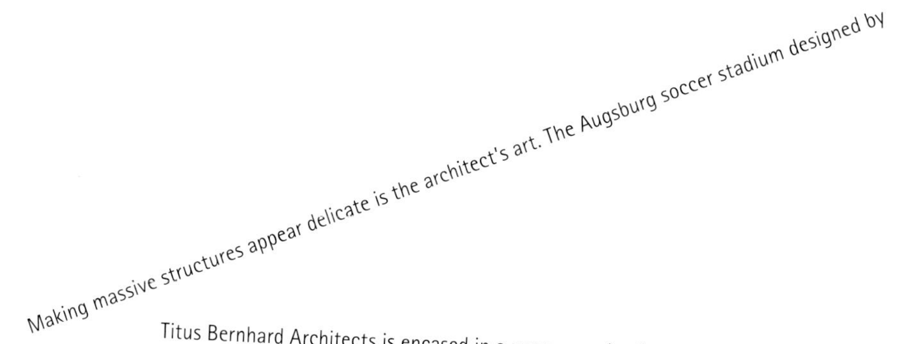

Making massive structures appear delicate is the architect's art. The Augsburg soccer stadium designed by Titus Bernhard Architects is encased in a woven mesh of round aluminum rods. There are also 170 lighting rods made from PLEXIGLAS® integrated into the weave. With some of them reaching up to eight meters in length, these tubes ensure not only great lighting effects, but also static stability.

Große Bauten filigran wirken zu lassen, ist die Kunst von Architekten. Die Augsburger Fußballarena von Titus Bernhard Architekten ist eingehüllt in ein Geflecht aus Aluminium-rundstäben. Darin sind auch 170 Leuchtstäbe aus PLEXIGLAS® konstruktiv verwoben: Mit bis zu acht Metern Länge sorgen die Rohre nicht nur für große Lichteffekte, sondern auch für statische Stabilität.

Garten

With

6,900 panels of

15-millimeter PLEXIGLAS®

Julius Berger gave the Godswill Akpabio

International Stadium in Nigeria an unmistakable look.

The triangular panels with a satin surface on both sides, produce a

distinctive pattern and permanently stay white even under

the hot African sun as the chemical composition

of the material makes it thoroughly

UV stable.

Mit 6.900 Platten aus 15 Millimeter dickem PLEXIGLAS® hat Julius Berger dem Godswill Akpabio International Stadium in Nigeria einen unverwechselbaren Charakter verliehen. Die dreieckigen, beidseitig satinierten Platten erzeugen ein markantes Muster und bleiben auch unter der heißen Sonne Afrikas dauerhaft weiß, da das Material aufgrund seines chemischen Aufbaus durch und durch UV-stabil ist.

The Lateralo pendant luminaire,
designed for TRILUX by Hartmut S. Engel, compels you to wonder where the
light is coming from? This new form of lighting aesthetics has been made possible by parallel developments in the worlds of technology
and materials: the point lighting from ultra-flat LEDs is fed into a PLEXIGLAS® light guide, and uniformly diffused through microstructures.

Bei der Pendelleuchte Lateralo, die Hartmut S. Engel für TRILUX entworfen hat, stellt sich unwillkürlich die Frage: Woher kommt das Licht? Diese neue Form der Lichtästhetik konnte durch die parallele Weiterentwicklung von Technik und Material entstehen: Das Punktlicht ultraflacher LEDs wird in einen Lichtleiter aus PLEXIGLAS® eingekoppelt und durch Mikrostrukturen ganz gleichmäßig gestreut.

The LED pendant luminaire Transparency was created based on a design by SCHMITZ | WILA. Its "restrained" design forms a framework in which light appears as an intricate screen. The frame contains a pane of PLEXIGLAS®, and appears almost empty when the light is switched off. When switched on, the empty space is uniformly filled with light, ensuring a dazzle-free and aesthetically sophisticated solution for the office.

Die LED-Pendelleuchte Transparency entstand nach einem Entwurf von SCHMITZ | WILA. Ihre zurückgenommene Gestaltung bildet den Rahmen, in dem Licht als filigrane Leinwand erscheint: In ausgeschaltetem Zustand wirkt der Rahmen, in dem eine Scheibe aus PLEXIGLAS® liegt, fast leer. Im eingeschalteten Zustand füllt sich diese Leere gleichmäßig mit Licht und sorgt für eine blendfreie und ästhetisch anspruchsvolle Lösung im Büro.

LED technology has ushered in a new age in lighting: longer-lasting, thinner, more efficient. For their energy efficiency to come into its own, however, LEDs require materials that can distribute their point lighting over a wider area without significant losses. For its desk luminaires, luminaire manufacturer MAUL uses diffusion plates made from diffuse light-scattering PLEXIGLAS®, which ensures the glare-free distribution of light.

Die LED-Technik hat eine neue Licht-Ära begründet: langlebiger, schlanker, sparsamer. Damit ihre Energiebilanz aufgeht, benötigen LEDs aber Materialien, die ihr Punktlicht nahezu verlustfrei in die Fläche tragen. Der Leuchtenhersteller MAUL setzt bei seinen Schreibtischleuchten auf Streuscheiben aus diffus lichtstreuendem PLEXIGLAS®, das für eine blendfreie Lichtverteilung sorgt.

The Thermomix is the undisputed number 1, multifunctional kitchen appliance. In order to visually underscore its status as market leader, the manufacturer Vorwerk makes use of a surface finish made from PLEXIGLAS®, with a brilliant depth effect. It is resistant to many chemicals and cleaning agents, and thus extends the useful lifetime of the appliance.

Der Thermomix ist unbestritten die Nummer 1 unter den multifunktionalen Küchengeräten. Damit er auch optisch seinen Führungsanspruch unterstreicht, setzt Hersteller Vorwerk auf eine Oberflächenveredelung aus PLEXIGLAS® mit brillanter Tiefenwirkung. Sie ist beständig gegen viele Chemikalien und Reinigungsmittel und verlängert damit seine Nutzungs- und Lebensdauer.

THE
BASIC
COOK
BOOK

VORWERK

Menu
00 00
min : sec
°C
0

As smooth as a water-polished pebble, combined with all the function of a touchpad: the interface in the Mercedes E-Class needs to withstand millions of contacts, and be resistant to sweat, creams and finger rings. To meet these high requirements, the component has been manufactured using the CoverForm® process, where the PLEXIGLAS® is equipped with a specially developed scratch-proof coating while still in the injection molding tool.

Das haptische Erlebnis eines Handschmeichlers und die Funktion eines Touchpads: Das Interface in der E-Klasse von Mercedes muss millionenfache Berührung aushalten und unempfindlich gegen Schweiß, Creme oder Ringe am Finger sein. Für diese hohe Anforderung wurde das Bauteil im CoverForm®-Verfahren hergestellt, bei dem das PLEXIGLAS® bereits im Spritzgießwerkzeug mit einer eigens entwickelten Kratzfestbeschichtung ausgestattet wird.

MEDIA
TEL
ON
VOL

A distinctive feature of the current model range from Opel is the concise, arrow-shaped light signature of the LED rear lights. A new PLEXIGLAS® diffuser molding compound allows rear lights utilizing these surface light guide to be designed even flatter, without the appearance of disturbing light hotspots. The smaller installation depth results in a larger trunk space for the customer.

Ein Erkennungszeichen der aktuellen Modellpalette von Opel ist die prägnante, pfeilförmige Lichtsignatur der LED-Rückleuchten. Eine neue PLEXIGLAS® Diffuser-Formmasse ermöglicht es, Heckleuchten mit solchen Flächenlichtleitern flacher auszuführen, ohne dass störende Licht-Hotspots zu sehen sind. Aus der geringeren Einbautiefe resultiert für die Kunden ein größerer Kofferraum.

Making complex technology simple is what designers do. Light and thermo-management, color standards and weathering resistance are the reasons why ten different kinds of PLEXIGLAS® components are integrated into each rear light of the BMW 5 series - but none of that is visible to the naked eye. The clear, sharp lines of the BMW 5 series rear lights are striking.

Komplexe Technik einfach zu gestalten, ist die Aufgabe von Designern. Dass Licht- und Thermomanagement, Farbnormen oder auch Witterungsbeständigkeit Gründe dafür sind, in jede Rückleuchte des BMW 5er zehn PLEXIGLAS® Teile unterschiedlicher Typen zu integrieren, sieht man nicht. Die Rückleuchten des BMW 5er bestechen durch ihre klare und scharfe Linie.

XDrive

530d

LED rear lights in a Union Jack design from the BMW Group. MINI is celebrating the 60th anniversary of the brand with an exclusive design model. Specific design features like the rear lights made from PLEXIGLAS® emphasize the British flair of the compact car, underlining with symbolic and communicative significance of design with a nod to the origins of the original. *LED-Heckleuchten im Union-Jack-Design der BMW Group. MINI feiert das 60-jährige Bestehen der Marke mit einem exklusiven Designmodell. Spezifische Gestaltungsmerkmale wie die Heckleuchten aus PLEXIGLAS® betonen das britische Flair des Kleinwagens und unterstreichen mit dem Hinweis auf die Herkunft des Originals die symbolische und kommunikative Bedeutung von Design.*

MINI

FORM FOLLOWS RELIABILITY

PLEXIGLAS® OFFERS LASTING PERFORMANCE

Designers, architects and companies count on materials that give their creations and products a reliably high-quality appearance. Aggressive UV radiation, humidity and frequent cleaning makes most plastics look rough, dull and, ultimately, unsightly.

PLEXIGLAS®, on the other hand, is weather-resistant and UV stable. In other words, not only the surface, but the entire material is protected from the damaging effect of the sun's radiation. This allows translucent façade elements permanently to retain their first-class visual appearance and, contrary to other plastics, also maintain higher transparency levels. Exterior lighting on streets, squares or sports sites does not lose its brightness over decades for the same reason.

PLEXIGLAS® is furthermore abrasion resistant as it has the highest surface hardness of all thermoplastics. This is why jet-black car pillar covers, for instance, are not only insensitive to sunlight, but also to repeated visits to the car wash.

PLEXIGLAS® ÜBERZEUGT DAUERHAFT

Designer, Architekten und Unternehmen setzen auf Materialien, die ihren Entwürfen und Produkten zuverlässig ein hochwertiges Erscheinungsbild ermöglichen. Doch aggressive UV-Strahlen, Feuchtigkeit und häufiges Reinigen lassen die allermeisten Kunststoffe rau, trübe und schließlich unansehnlich werden.

PLEXIGLAS® hingegen ist witterungsbeständig sowie durch und durch UV-stabil. Das heißt: Nicht nur die Oberfläche, sondern das gesamte Material ist gegen die schädliche Wirkung der Sonnenstrahlen geschützt. Dadurch behalten beispielsweise transluzente Fassadenelemente dauerhaft ihren hochwertigen optischen Ausdruck und auch ihre – im Vergleich zu anderen Kunststoffen höhere – Lichtdurchlässigkeit. Auch Außenbeleuchtungen für Straßen, Plätze oder Sportgelände büßen so für Jahrzehnte ihre Leuchtkraft nicht ein.

Darüber hinaus ist PLEXIGLAS® abriebbeständig – weil es die höchste Oberflächenhärte aller thermoplastischen Kunststoffe aufweist. Auf diese Weise werden zum Beispiel tiefschwarze Säulenblenden von Autos nicht nur unempfindlich gegenüber Sonnenlicht, sondern auch gegenüber häufigen Besuchen in der Waschanlage.

Good, clear lighting guarantees safety. The Floodlight 20 system from SITECO works with 15 different combinations of LEDs and lenses to ensure the safest result for every application, avoiding glare, hard shadows and high-contrast zones. Precise light control is delivered by PLEXIGLAS® lenses.

Eine klare, gute Beleuchtung ist der Garant für Sicherheit. Das Flutersystem Floodlight 20 von SITECO arbeitet mit 15 unterschiedlichen LED/Linsen-Kombinationen, sodass für jeden Anwendungsfall das sicherste Ergebnis erzielt wird: ohne Blendung, Schlagschatten oder Hell-Dunkel-Zonen. Die präzise Lichtlenkung übernehmen Linsen aus PLEXIGLAS®. Design: SITECO.

IN AQ6050
A6
allroad

The arrow-shaped signature light guides in the split rear light of the Audi A6 are made from PLEXIGLAS® Satinice, which ensures homogeneous light distribution and avoids hotspots. The cover is manufactured from signal red PLEXIGLAS®. Together, these materials reliably contribute to greater safety in road traffic, ensuring the signal functions are easily seen.

Bei der zweigeteilten Rückleuchte des Audi A6 besteht der pfeilförmige Signatur-Lichtleiter aus PLEXIGLAS® Satinice, das für eine homogene Lichtverteilung sorgt und Hotspots vermeidet. Die Abdeckscheibe ist aus PLEXIGLAS® in Signalrot gefertigt. Zusammen tragen die Werkstoffe zuverlässig zu mehr Sicherheit im Straßenverkehr bei, indem die Signalfunktionen gut wahrgenommen werden können. Design: AUDI.

BZ15 DEF

It was a turning point in automotive design: the year 2000 was the first year in which MINI used pillar covers that no longer needed to be painted after injection molding. They were made from high-gloss, jet black PLEXIGLAS® that is colored right through the material. By eliminating the additional production step of painting, the manufacturing process became significantly more cost-effective: premium quality for the premium brand MINI.

Es war eine Wende im Automobilbau: Im Jahr 2000 verwendete MINI erstmals Säulenblenden, die nach dem Spritzgießen nicht lackiert werden mussten. Sie bestanden aus hochglänzendem, durchgefärbtem, tiefschwarzem PLEXIGLAS®. Durch den Wegfall des zusätzlichen Produktionsschritts der Lackierung wurde die Herstellung deutlich wirtschaftlicher: Premiumqualität für die Premiummarke MINI. Design: BMW Group.

The Touareg is the premium model from Volkswagen. It redefines the whole concept of the luxury vehicle. The C pillar cover made from jet black, high-gloss PLEXIGLAS® underscores this quality claim, and contributes to the glass-like appearance with its elegant and luxurious aesthetic, visually increasing the size of the windows.

Der Touareg ist das Premiummodell von Volkswagen. Er definiert das Thema „Oberklasse und Luxus“ neu. Die C-Säulenblende aus tiefschwarzem, hochglänzendem PLEXIGLAS® unterstreicht diesen Qualitätsanspruch und trägt durch die glasähnliche Anmutung zu einer eleganten und luxuriösen Ästhetik mit optisch vergrößerten Fenstern bei. Design: Volkswagen.

The territory of an SUV like the Volkswagen T-Roc extends far beyond the road. But driving through the wilds can place extremely high demands on the material. The PLEXIGLAS® pillar covers not only have a high surface hardness that makes them very robust, but are also colored right through the material, meaning small chips and scratches do not attract attention, and can even be completely removed by polishing.

Das Revier eines SUVs wie des T-Roc von Volkswagen geht weit über die Straße hinaus. Doch eine Fahrt durchs Gelände stellt hohe Anforderungen an das Material. Die Säulenblenden aus PLEXIGLAS® haben nicht nur eine hohe Oberflächenhärte und sind damit robust, sie sind auch durchgefärbt, sodass kleine Steinschläge oder Kratzer nicht auffallen und sogar herauspoliert werden können. Design: Volkswagen.

WOB TR 106

The elegance of a sedan car like the Opel Insignia comes from its proportions, and the contrast between light and shade. In order to ensure this elegance stands the test of time, Opel uses long-lasting materials. The high-gloss B pillar covers made from the jet black PLEXIGLAS® Piano Black are also totally insensitive to UV radiation and mechanical loading.

Die Eleganz einer Limousine wie des Opel Insignia entsteht durch ihre Proportionen und den Kontrast von Licht und Schatten. Damit diese Eleganz viele Jahre überdauert, setzt Opel auf langlebige Materialien. Die hochglänzenden B-Säulenblenden aus tiefschwarzem PLEXIGLAS® Piano Black sind absolut unempfindlich gegenüber UV-Strahlung und mechanischer Beanspruchung. Design: Opel Automobile.

A curtain that moves without moving hangs in front of the London head office of the Reiss fashion label. It is composed of PLEXIGLAS® panels, which have been milled out, matted or polished to break the light in different ways, creating the impression that the curtain is fluttering. PLEXIGLAS® was also the material of choice because it is stable and does not yellow.

Ein Vorhang, der sich bewegt, ohne sich zu bewegen, hängt vor der Londoner Zentrale des Modelabels Reiss. Er besteht aus PLEXIGLAS® Paneelen, die unterschiedlich ausgefräst, mattiert oder poliert wurden, sodass sich das Licht auf vielfältige Weise bricht und den Vorhang vermeintlich wallen lässt. PLEXIGLAS® war auch deshalb das Material der Wahl, weil es stabil ist und nicht vergilbt.

Architecture | Architektur: Squire and Partner.

When open, the folding sliding shutters of the Raiffeisen Regionalbank Hall in Tirol, Austria, resemble a row of flags pointing outwards. When closed, the PLEXIGLAS® Satinice sun protection immerses the interior in pleasant light with reduced UV radiation. The weather-resistant folding sliding shutters can be individually adjusted for the 18 façade sections, continuously changing the aesthetic appearance of the building.

Geöffnet ragen die Faltschiebeläden der Raiffeisen Regionalbank Hall in Tirol wie aufgereihte Fahnen nach außen, geschlossen taucht der Sonnenschutz aus PLEXIGLAS® Satinice die Räume in angenehmes Licht mit verminderter UV-Strahlung. Die witterungsbeständigen Faltschiebeläden können für die 18 Fassadenflächen individuell eingestellt werden und geben dem Gebäude immer wieder eine neue Ästhetik.

Architecture | Architektur: AO-Architekten ZT, Photo | Foto: Raiffeisen Regionalbank Hall in Tirol.

The Kunsthaus Graz was designed by architects Peter Cook and Colin Fournier, and is a landmark of the city and an artwork in itself. Its amorphous shell is composed of 1,068 transparent blue PLEXIGLAS® panels, which were individually shaped in three dimensions. Behind the panels are almost nine hundred square meters of luminaires, which can be individually activated like pixels. This makes the façade the biggest screen in the city.

Das Kunsthaus Graz der Architekten Peter Cook und Colin Fournier ist Wahrzeichen der Stadt und selbst ein Kunstwerk. Seine amorphe Hülle formt sich aus 1.068 blautransparenten PLEXIGLAS® Platten, die einzeln dreidimensional verformt wurden. Hinter ihnen sitzen auf 900 Quadratmetern Lampen, die wie Pixel einzeln angesteuert werden können. Dadurch wird die Fassade zur größten Leinwand der Stadt.

Architecture | Architektur: Peter Cook, Colin Fournier.

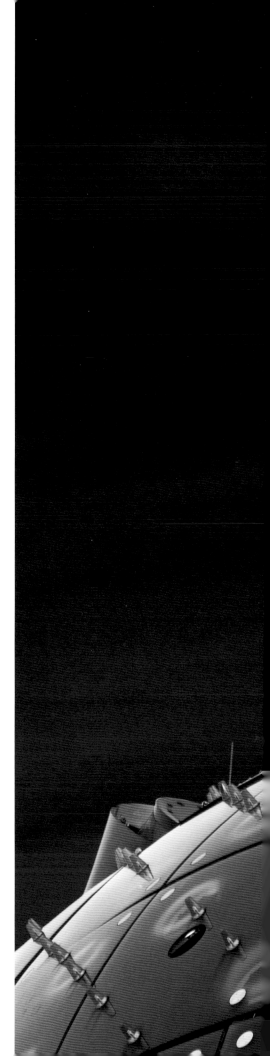

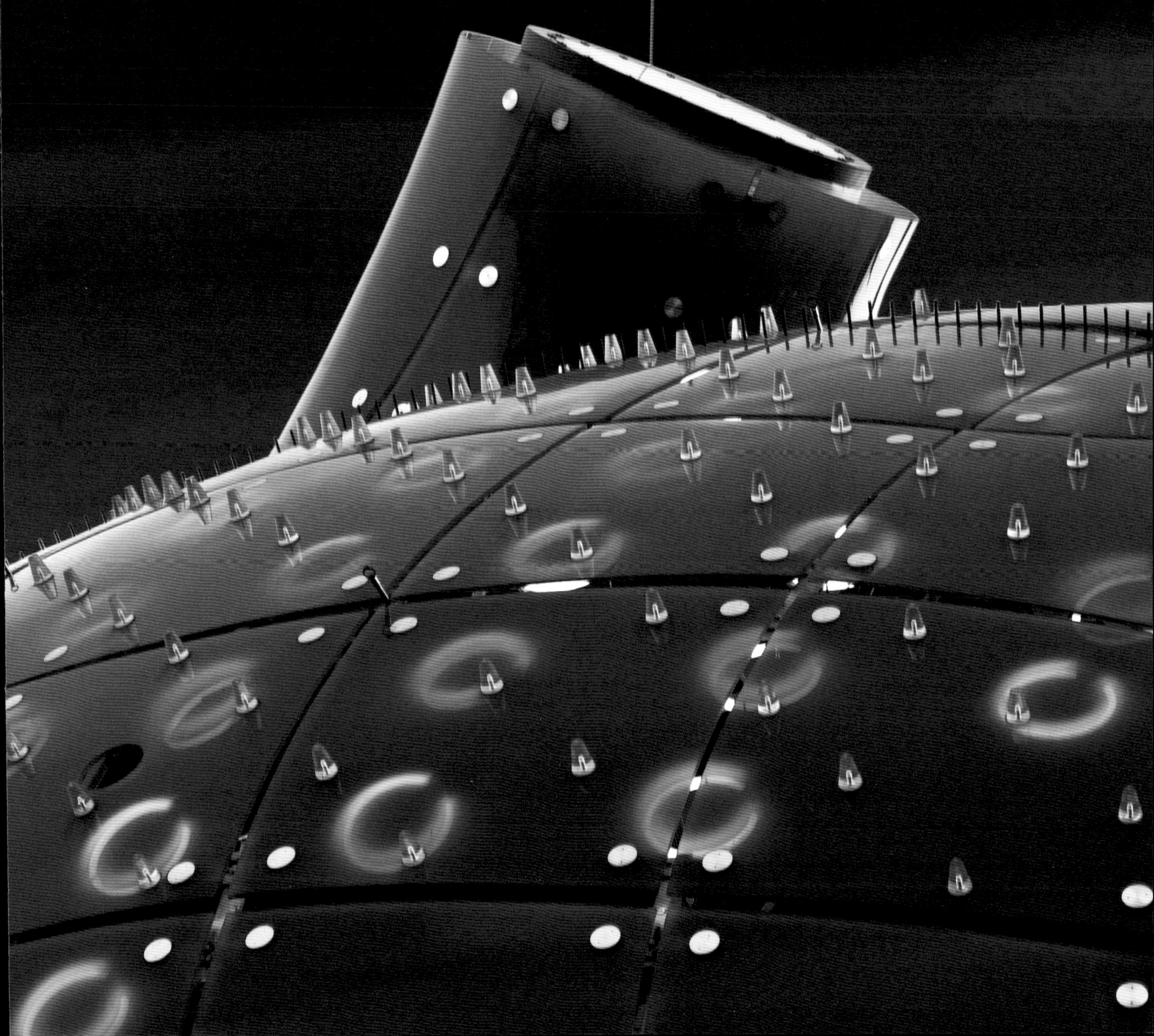

Virtually frameless inside, colorful outside. The innovative profile structure of plastic-framed windows gives architects greater design freedom. In order to make these colored profiles more weather-resistant, GEALAN fits its profiles with a surface finish made from UV-resistant PLEXIGLAS®. PVC and PMMA are inseparably bound together in a single process step known as coextrusion.

Innen quasi rahmenlos, außen farbig: Ein innovativer Profilaufbau von Kunststofffenstern gibt Architekten mehr Gestaltungsfreiheit. Um diese farbigen Profile witterungsbeständiger zu machen, stattet GEALAN seine Profile mit einer Oberflächenveredelung aus UV-beständigem PLEXIGLAS® aus. PVC und PMMA werden dazu in einem einzigen Prozessschritt durch Coextrusion untrennbar miteinander verbunden.

Design: GEALAN Fenster-Systeme.

The 'Split and Store' from the Dutch design studio RENS combines a room divider and a shelving unit to solve two problems at once, simultaneously partitioning a room and providing storage space. Prominent in the simple design is the color of the PLEXIGLAS® Satinice sliding doors. Because the material itself is completely colorless, it can be colored to exact specifications.

Split and Store, die Einheit aus Raumteiler und Regal des niederländischen Designstudios RENS, löst zwei Probleme auf einmal: Es ist Sichtschutz und Stauraum zugleich. Schlicht in der Form tritt die Farbe der Schiebetüren aus PLEXIGLAS® Satinice in den Vordergrund. Da das Material keinerlei Eigenfarbe besitzt, kann es exakt eingefärbt werden. Design: Studio RENS.

FORM FOLLOWS EMOTION

PLEXIGLAS® AROUSES PASSIONATE REACTIONS

Emotions are often difficult to describe in words. They are what catch hold of us when we feel something. That is also true of materials and the products that are made of them. Frequently, it is impossible to express in words what makes them appealing – but we are still gripped by emotion. In other words, our experience of a product is not influenced by rational reasons alone. The aesthetics of the material are, in fact, the non-verbal communication of design.

PLEXIGLAS® awakens precisely these emotions. It gives furniture, for example, a satin surface that has a pleasant feel, which can be experienced through touch. In the lighting sector, on the other hand, the material produces an atmospheric lighting ambience that is perceived as elegant and sophisticated.

Occasionally, PLEXIGLAS® can also lend wing to the imagination, for example when it projects beyond the façade of a hotel at dizzying heights as the base of a pool – an experience of swimming that is bound to stir the emotions.

PLEXIGLAS® WECKT LEIDENSCHAFT

Emotionen lassen sich nicht immer in Worten ausdrücken. Sie sind das, was uns ergreift, weil wir etwas spüren. Das trifft auch auf Materialien und die Produkte zu, die aus ihnen gefertigt werden. Häufig können wir nicht in Worte fassen, was uns an ihnen begeistert – aber die Emotion erfasst uns trotzdem. Das heißt: Wir erleben ein Produkt nicht nur über rationale Argumente. Vielmehr ist die Ästhetik des Materials die nonverbale Kommunikationsebene im Design.

PLEXIGLAS® weckt genau diese Emotionen. Möbeln beispielsweise verleiht der Werkstoff durch satinierte Oberflächen eine angenehme Haptik, die wir mit unseren Fingern erfühlen können. Bei Anwendungen im Zusammenhang mit Licht hingegen schafft das Material eine stimmungsvolle Lichtatmosphäre, die von uns als edel und hochwertig wahrgenommen wird.

Manchmal kann PLEXIGLAS® sogar die Fantasie beflügeln – dann, wenn es in luftiger Höhe als Boden eines Pools über die Fassade eines Hotels hinausragt: ein Badeerlebnis, das auf jeden Fall Emotionen weckt.

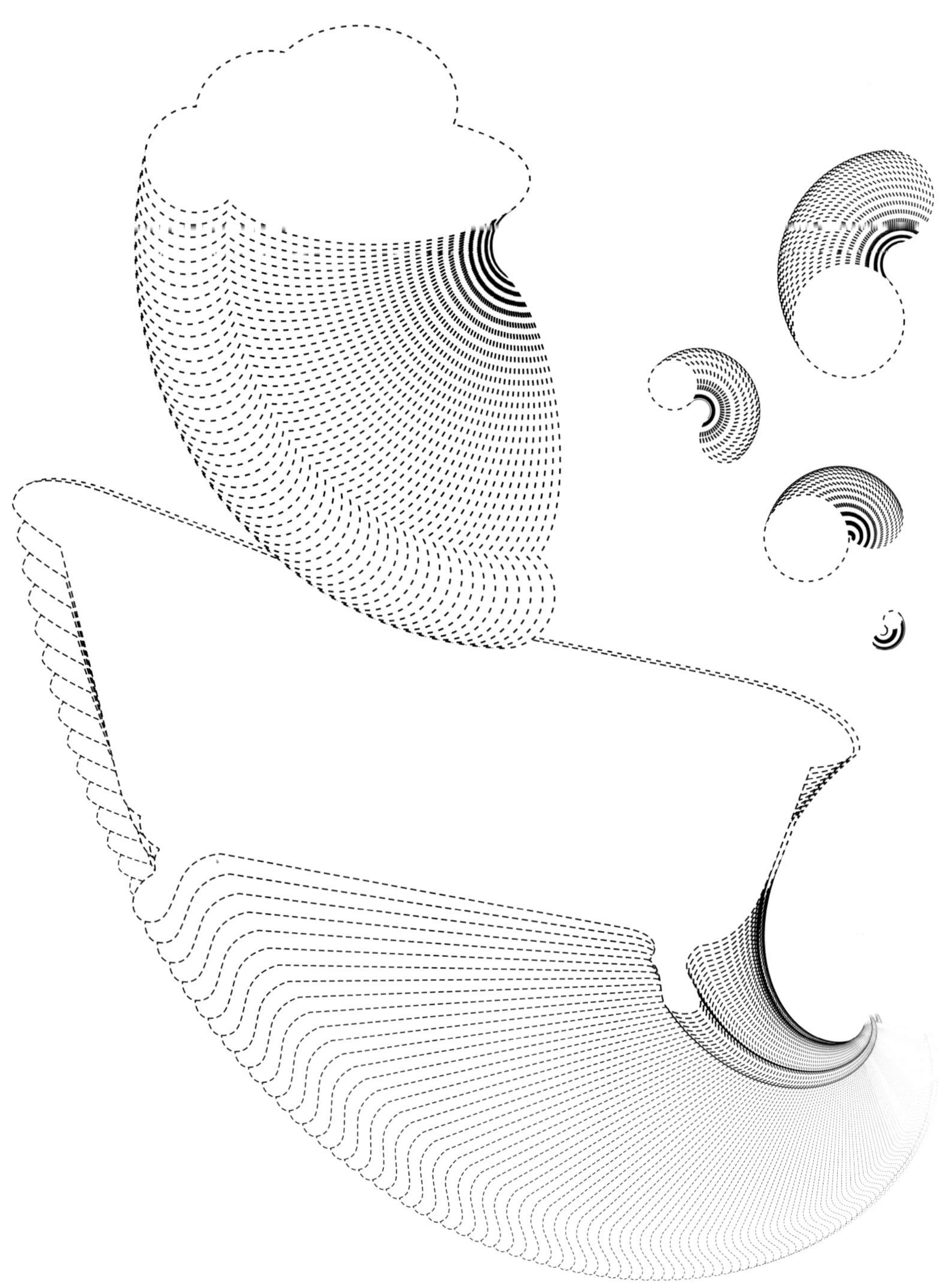

The imagination says,
"I want a bathtub that kisses
the sky."

PLEXIGLAS® says,
"Okay."

Die Fantasie sagt:
„Ich will eine Badewanne, die den
Himmel küsst!"

PLEXIGLAS® sagt:
„Okay."

Anyone who has stood on a 10-meter diving tower can imagine how high 50 meters must feel. On the 17th floor of the Hotel Clarion in Helsinki, the hotel pool projects five feet over the edge of the building. The bottom of the pool is made of PLEXIGLAS®, which despite its thickness is crystal clear, allowing a view of the long drop to the old Jätkäsaari Harbor below. Reassuringly, PLEXIGLAS® is extremely strong.

Wer schon einmal auf einem 10-Meter-Sprungturm stand, kann erahnen, wie hoch sich 50 Meter anfühlen müssen: Im 17. Stock des Hotels Clarion in Helsinki ragt der Hotelpool anderthalb Meter über die Gebäudekante hinaus. Sein Boden aus PLEXIGLAS®, der trotz der Dicke kristallklar ist, gibt den Blick in die Tiefe und auf den alten Hafen Jätkäsaari frei. Gut zu wissen, dass PLEXIGLAS® extrem bruchfest ist.

Photo | Foto: Berndorf Bäderbau, www.berndorf-baederbau.com.

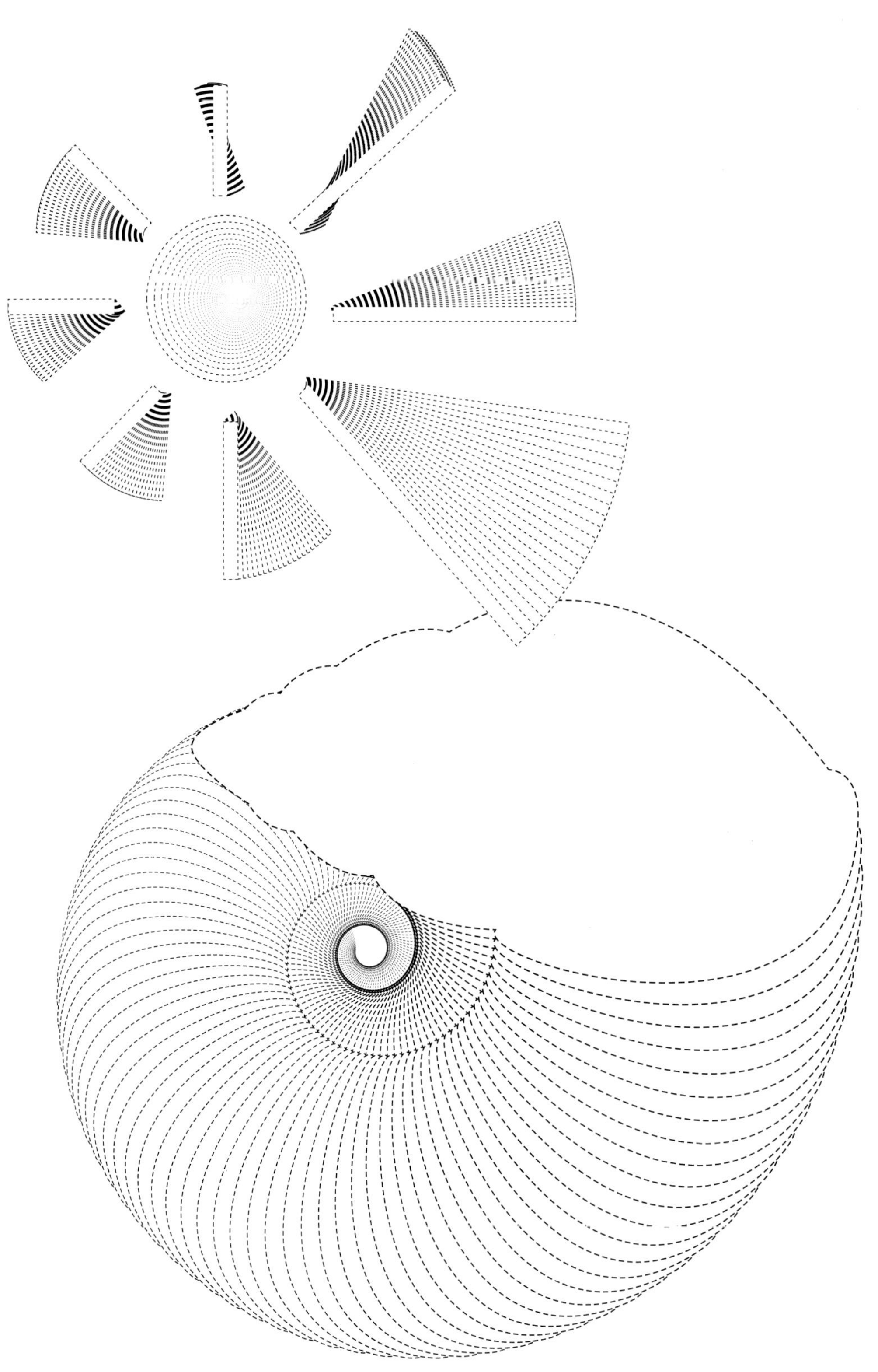

The imagination says,
"I want a snail's shell in which
I can see the sun."

PLEXIGLAS® says,
"All right."

Die Fantasie sagt:
„Ich will ein Schneckenhaus, in
dem ich die Sonne sehen kann!"

PLEXIGLAS® sagt:
„Geht klar."

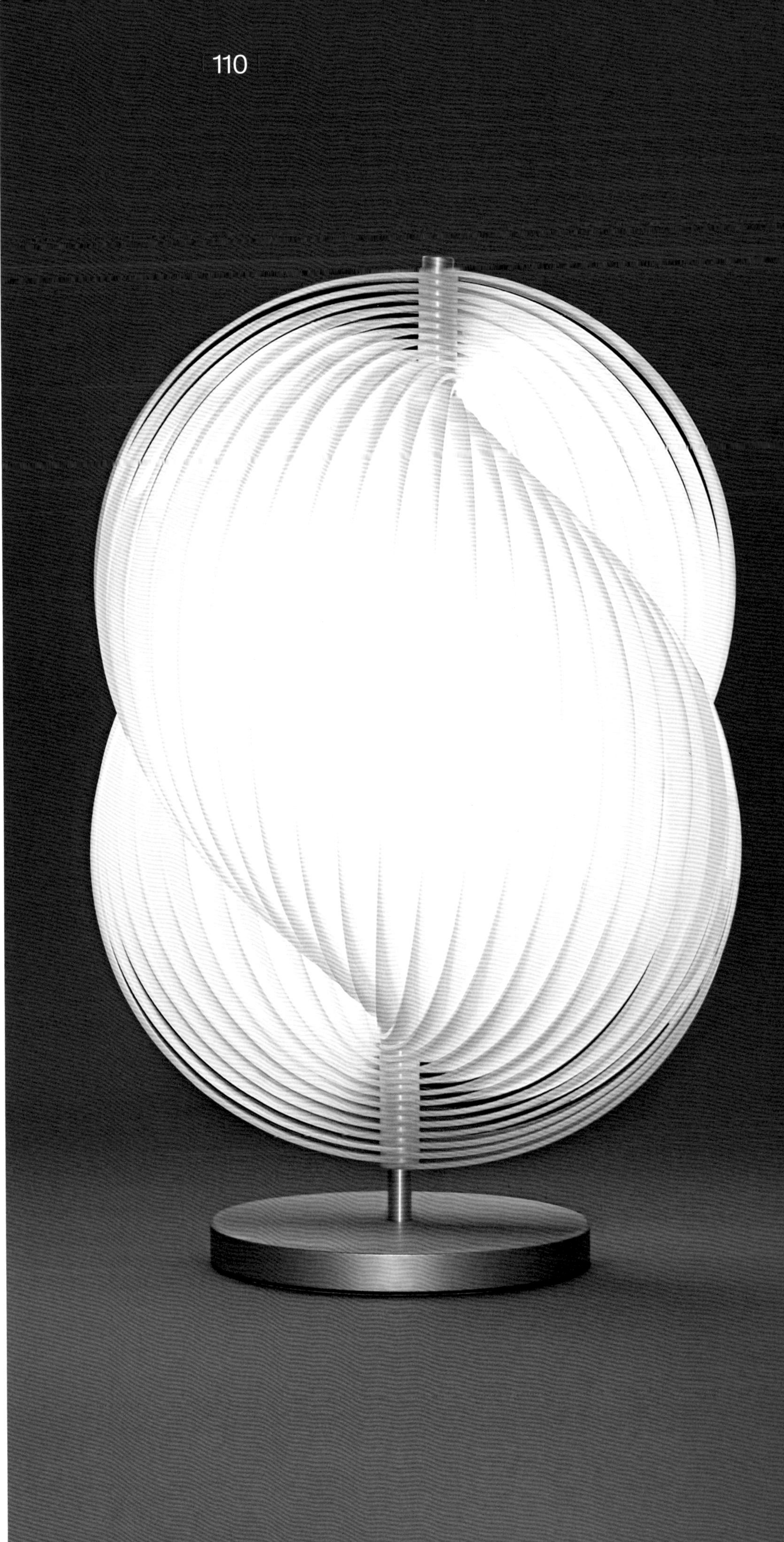

The Escargot2, La Perle and Mon Coeur luminaires designed by Nico Heilmann for the company Tecnolumen have a truly remarkable construction. The light is scattered by offset, heat-resistant PLEXIGLAS® slats, which form an organic shape and can be modified at will.

Die Leuchten Escargot2, La perle und Mon coeur, die der Designer Nico Heilmann für das Unternehmen Tecnolumen entworfen hat, zeichnen sich durch ihre besondere Konstruktion aus. Das Licht wird durch versetzt angeordnete, wärmebeständige PLEXIGLAS® Lamellen gestreut, die eine organische Form bilden und sich ganz nach Wunsch verändern lassen. Design: Nico Heilmann.

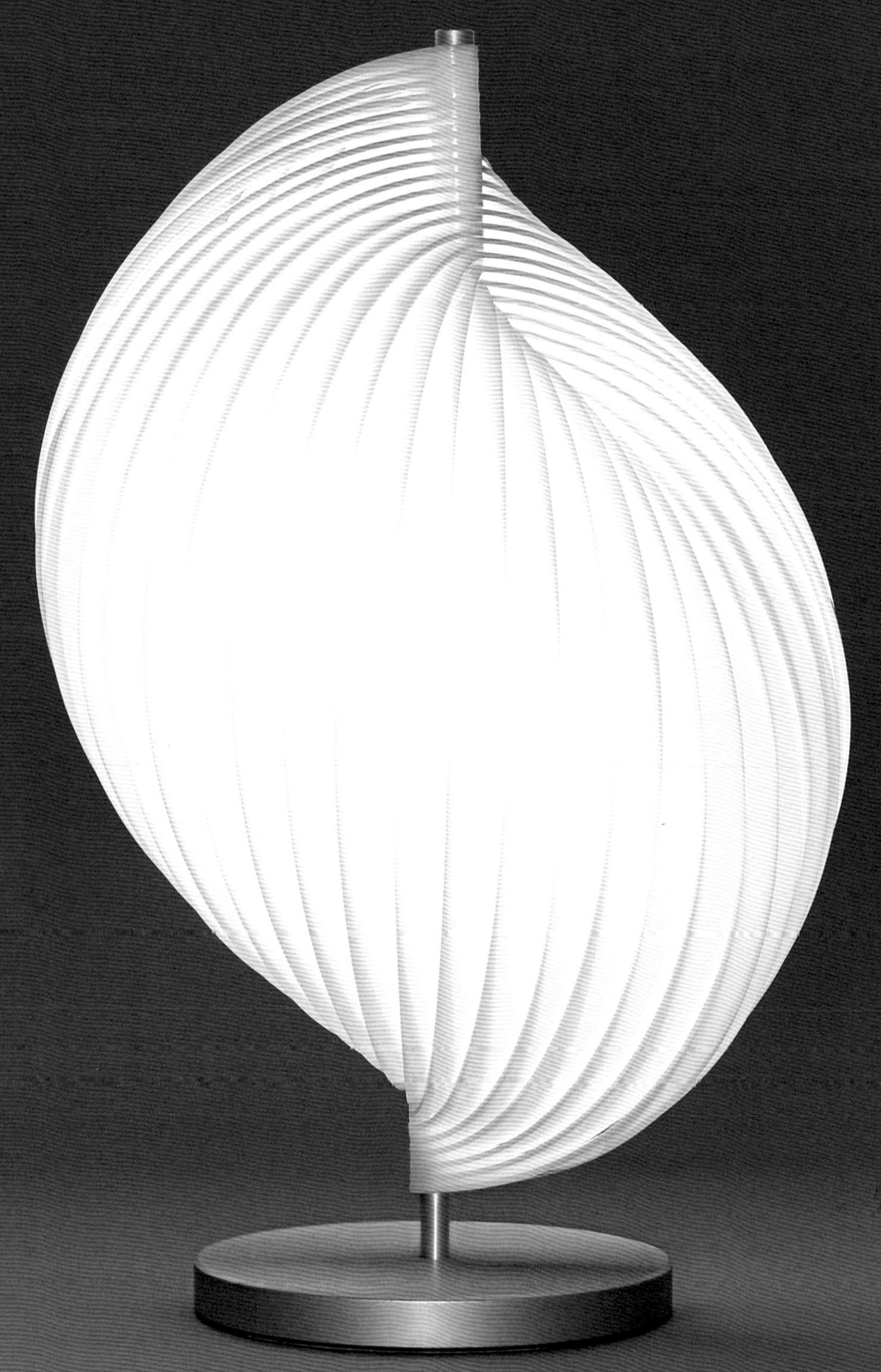

The imagination says,
"I want frozen lightning."

PLEXIGLAS® says,
"Certainly!"

Die Fantasie sagt:
„Ich will einen gefrorenen Blitz!"

PLEXIGLAS® sagt:
„Aber sicher doch."

Kundalini's Shakti luminaire range speaks the language of classic industrial design. The clear, simple forms of the extruded PLEXIGLAS® tubes derive their aesthetic value from the angle-cut ends, revealing the white interior. The columns are fitted with two bulbs, which are optionally available as halogen or fluorescent lamps. As a result of the coextrusion technology used, the luminaire always emits white light, even if a colored topcoat is selected.

Kundalinis Leuchtenserie Shakti spricht die Sprache klassischen Industriedesigns. Die einfachen, klaren Formen der extrudierten PLEXIGLAS® Rohre erhalten ihren ästhetischen Wert durch schräg angeschnittene Enden und geben den Blick auf die weiße Innenseite frei. Die Säulen sind mit zwei Glühlampen ausgestattet, wahlweise Halogen- oder Leuchtstofflampen. Aufgrund der verwendeten Coextrusionstechnologie gibt die Leuchte immer weißes Licht ab, auch wenn eine farbige Deckschicht gewählt wird. Design: Marzio Rusconi Clerici.

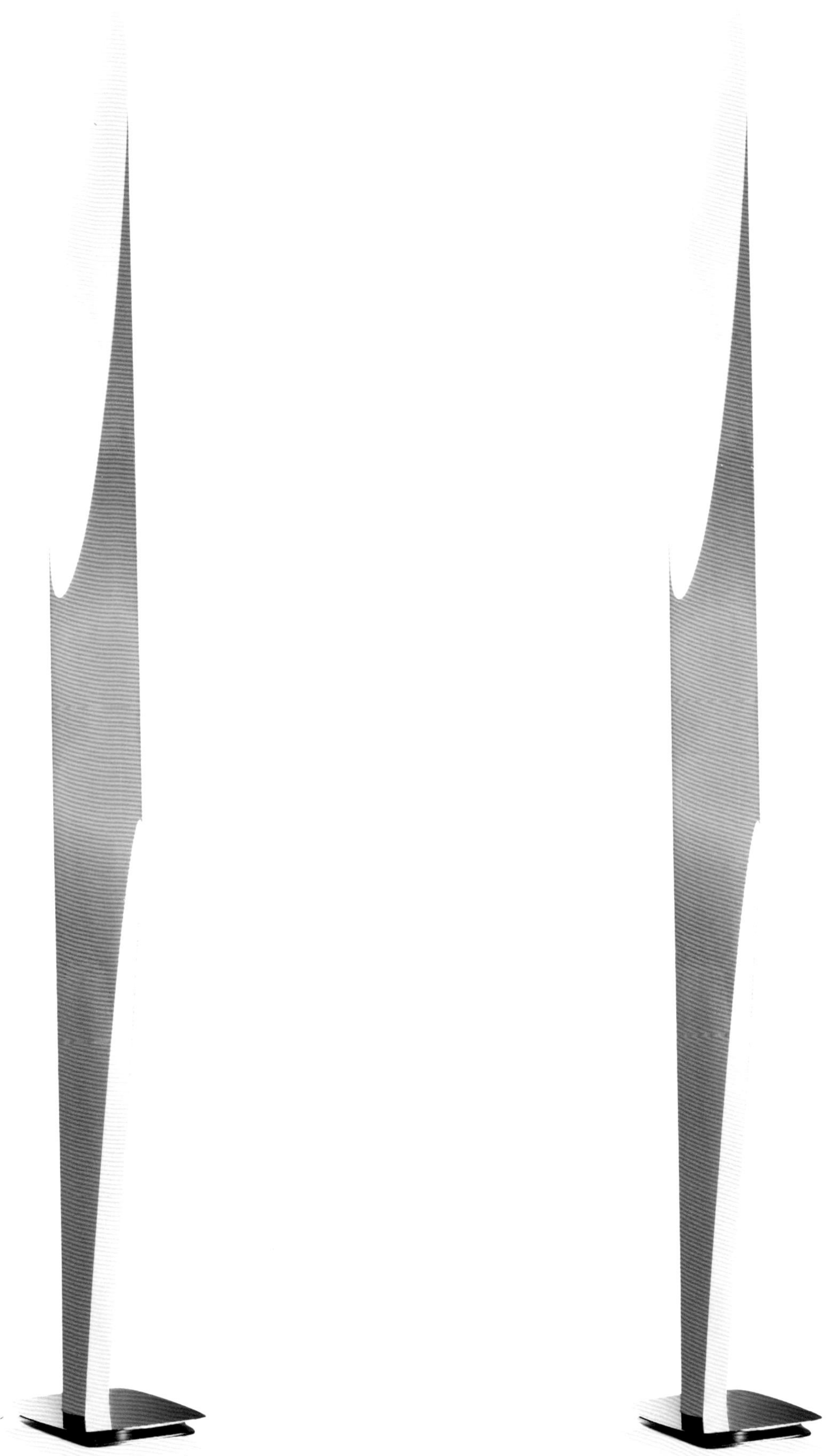

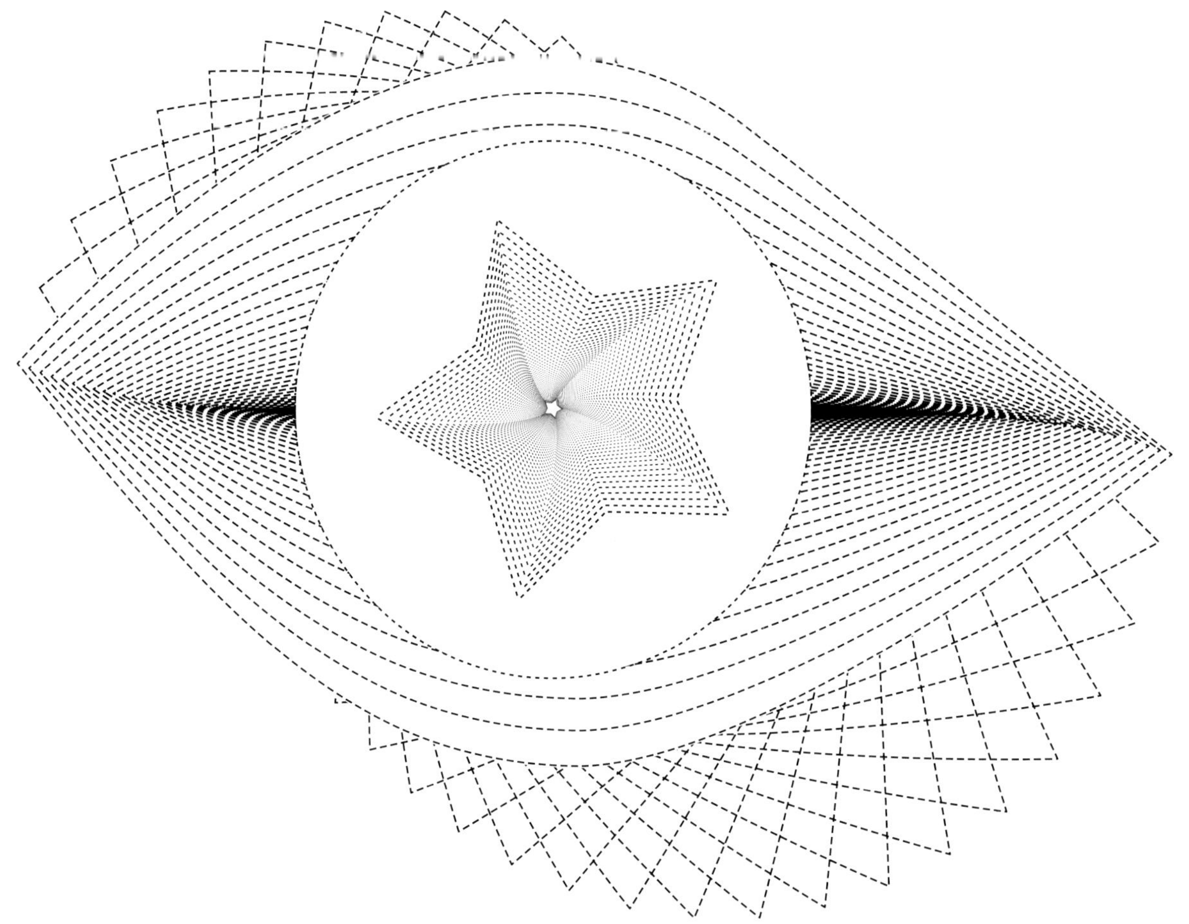

The imagination says,
“I want eyes that twinkle
like stars.”

PLEXIGLAS® says,
“But, of course!”

Die Fantasie sagt:
„Ich will Augen, die funkeln
wie die Sterne!“

PLEXIGLAS® sagt:
„Aber natürlich.“

The technical drive for progress is written all over the front end of the Mercedes-Benz C-Class. The clear sensual forms bring out the intelligent technology: the main headlamp and indicator lenses are made from PLEXIGLAS®, and the light guides for the daytime running light are made from PLEXIMID®, which has even higher heat resistance. Thanks to LED technology, they ensure top-end vision and visibility.

Der technische Vorwärtsdrang steht der Mercedes-Benz C-Klasse förmlich ins Gesicht geschrieben. Dabei lassen die sinnlich klaren Formen die intelligente Technik zum Vorschein kommen: Die Hauptscheinwerfer- und Blinkerlinsen bestehen aus PLEXIGLAS® und die Lichtleiter für das Tagfahrlicht aus PLEXIMID®, das über eine noch höhere Wärmeformbeständigkeit verfügt. Dank LED-Technologie bieten sie erstklassige Sicht und Sichtbarkeit. Design: Mercedes-Benz.

S MB 2501
AMG

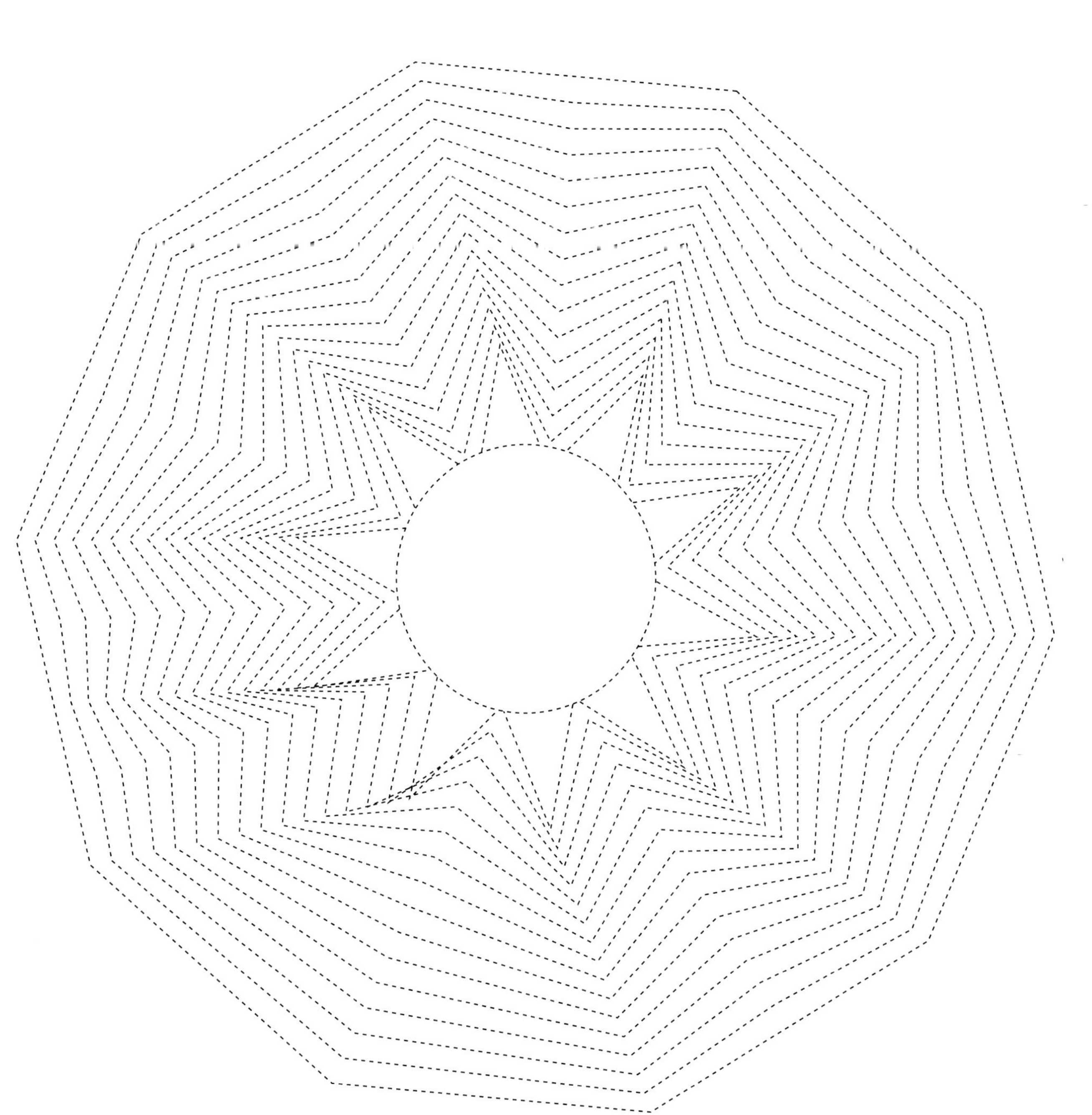

The imagination says,
"I want to sleep on a mesh of light."

PLEXIGLAS® says,
"With pleasure."

Die Fantasie sagt:
„Ich will auf einem Geflecht
aus Licht schlafen!"

PLEXIGLAS® sagt:
„Gerne."

The fascination of the lumiluxE lounge chair lies in its captivating technology. Thin lines are laser-engraved into its curvaceous PLEXIGLAS® surface. LED light is fed into its top edge and flows through the entire surface, but escapes only through the engravings. The result is striking: light itself becomes an object.

Die Faszination für den Lounge Chair lumiluxE liegt in der Faszination für seine Technik. In die geschwungene Liegefläche aus PLEXIGLAS® sind dünne Linien lasergraviert. Über die Oberkante wird LED-Licht eingeleitet, das durch die komplette Fläche fließt – doch nur an den gravierten Stellen tritt es aus. Das Ergebnis: Licht wird zum Objekt. Design: Axis.

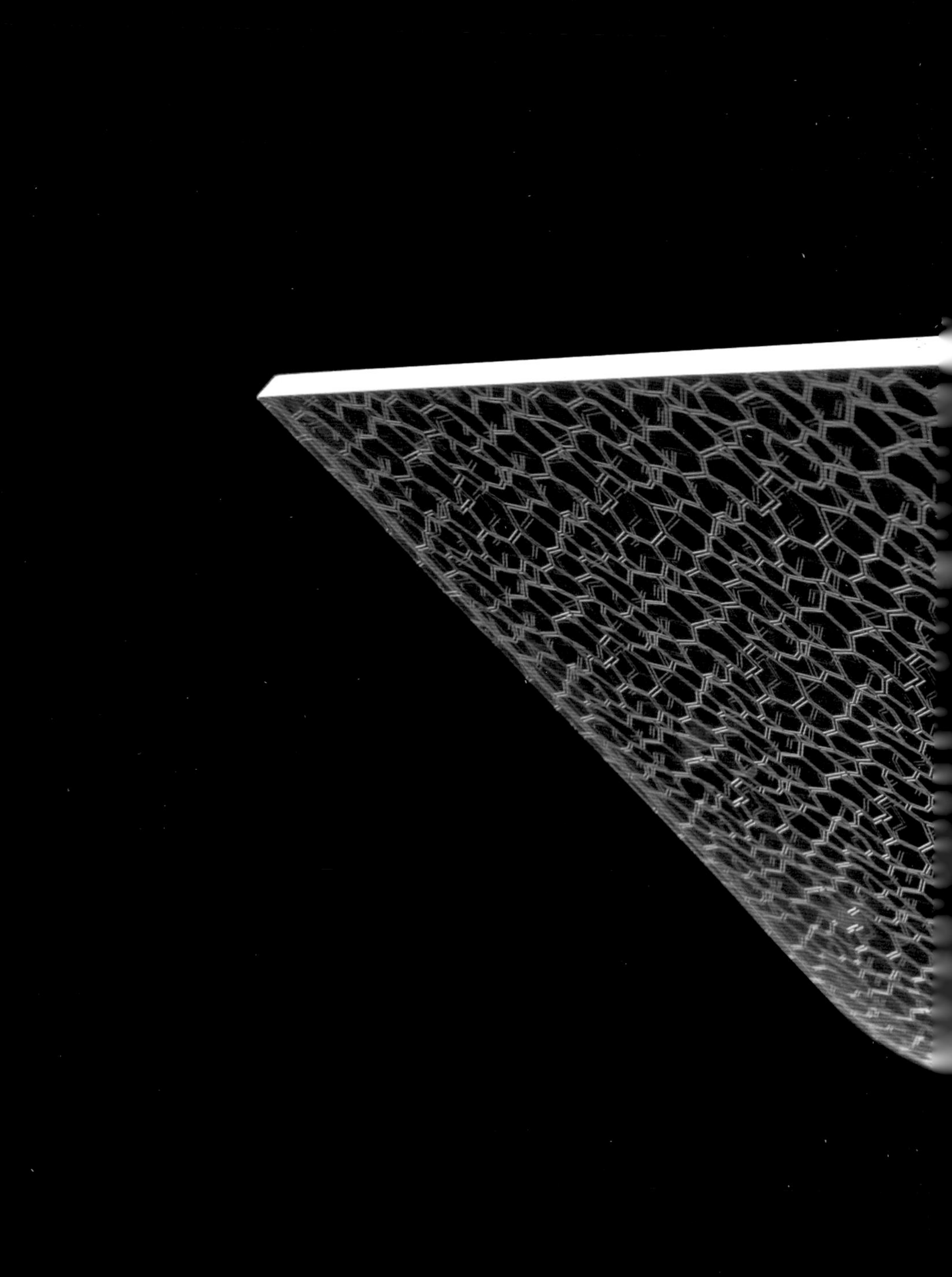

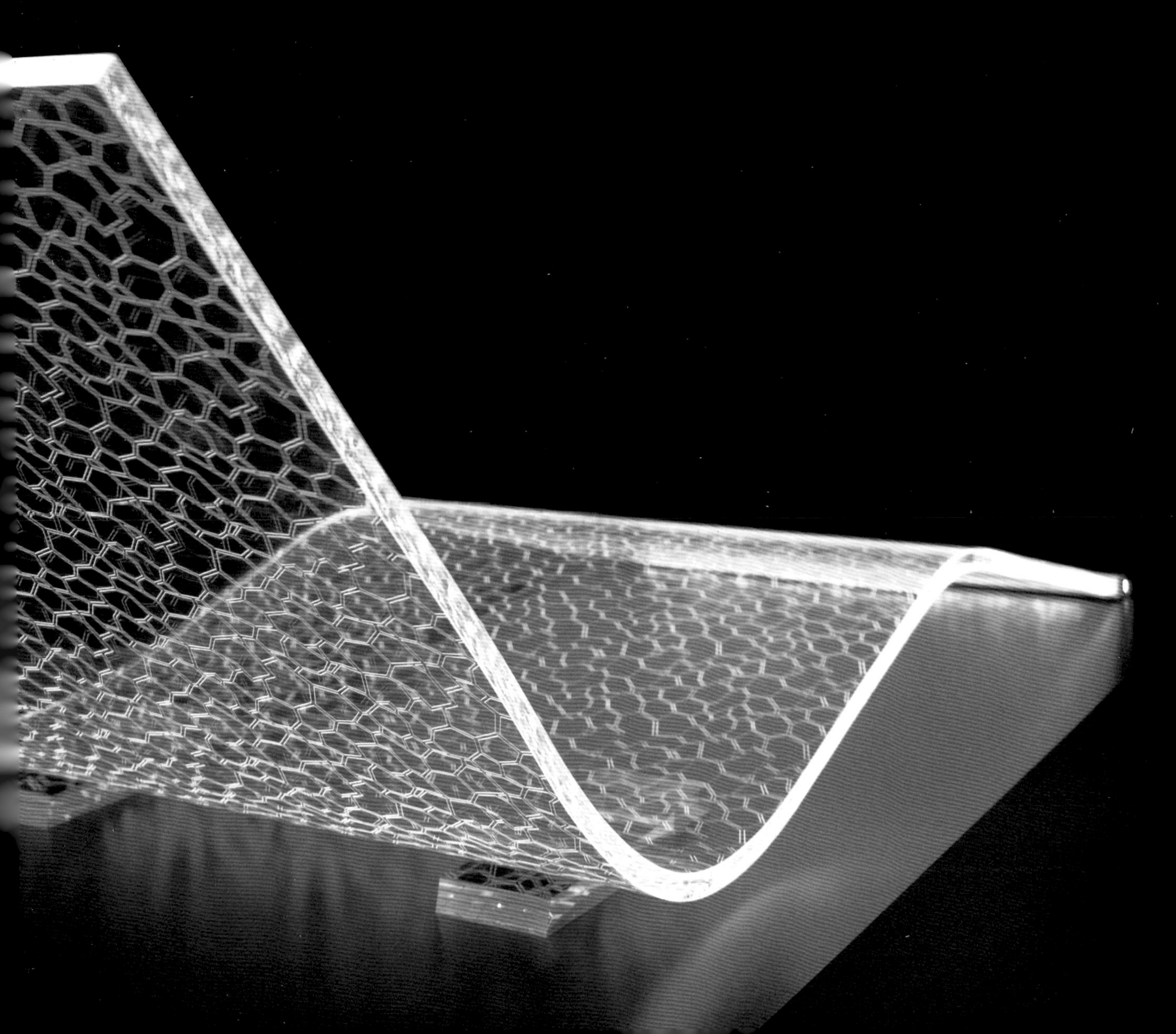

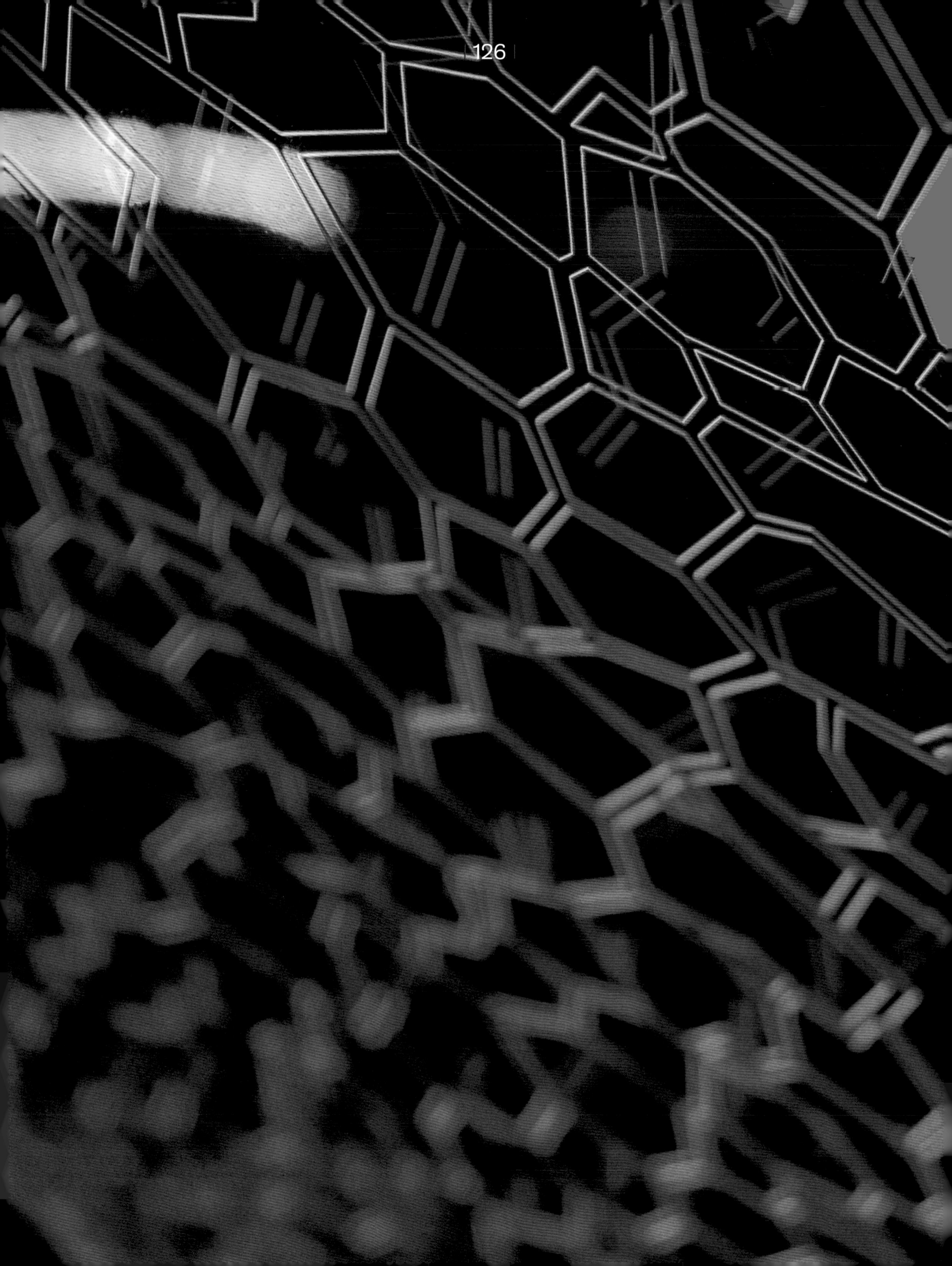

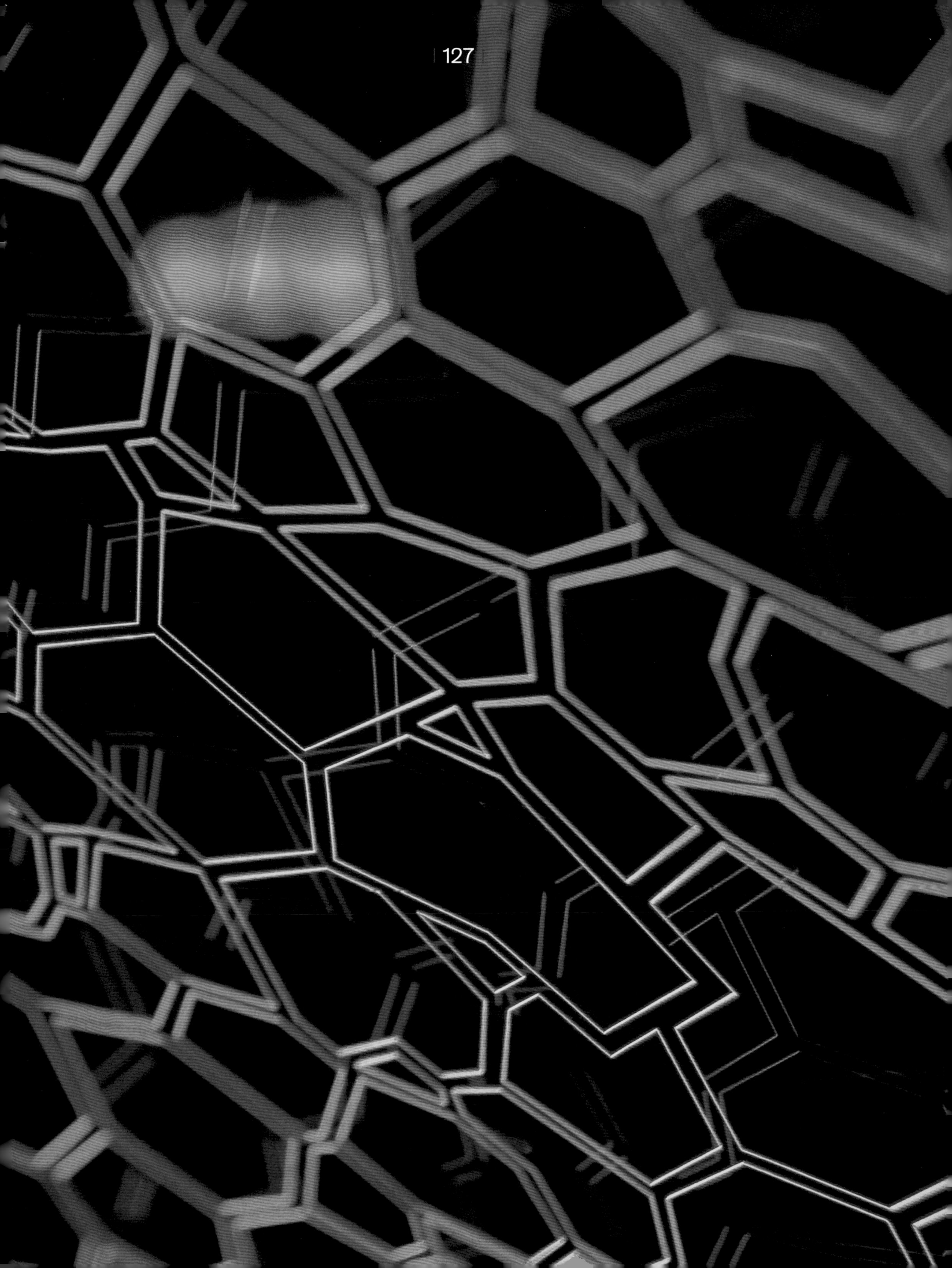

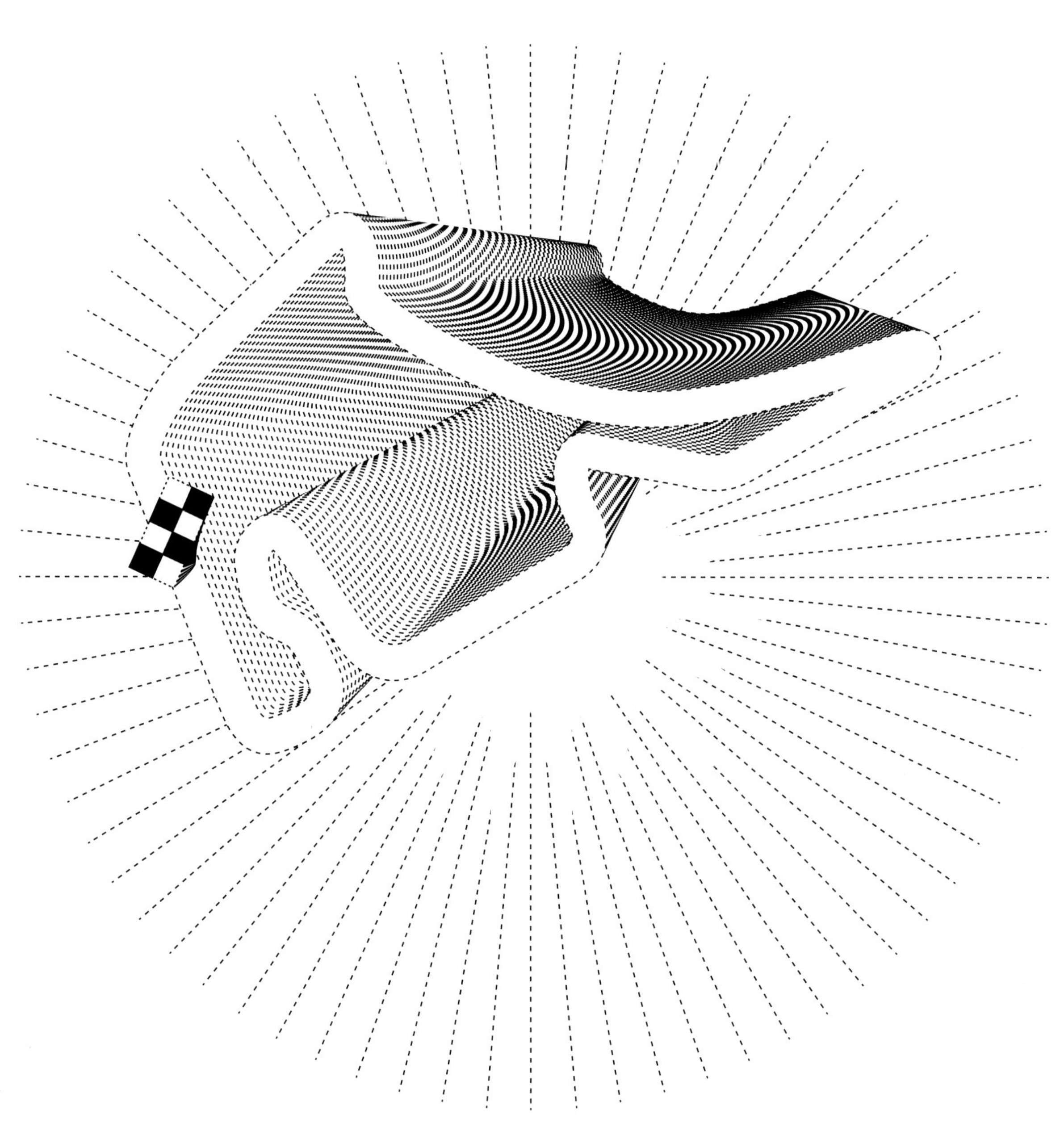

The imagination says,
"I want a racetrack for beams
of light."

PLEXIGLAS® says,
"Nothing could be easier."

Die Fantasie sagt:
„Ich will eine Rennstrecke
für Lichtstrahlen!"

PLEXIGLAS® sagt:
„Nichts leichter als das."

"Liviano" means lightweight, and the name for this pendant luminaire could scarcely be more appropriate, built as it is from transparency and light. The light flows into the entire plate of almost invisible PLEXIGLAS® and is coupled out along the engraved lines. This is also the reason why the young luminaire manufacturing business OCARI utilizes this material, whose excellent properties make it exceptionally well suited for the precise and intricate processing.

„Liviano" bedeutet „leicht". Und treffender hätte der Name für diese Pendelleuchte nicht sein können, denn sie besteht lediglich aus Transparenz und Licht. Das Licht fließt in eine Scheibe aus fast unsichtbarem PLEXIGLAS® und wird entlang der gravierten Linien ausgekoppelt. Die junge Leuchtenmanufaktur OCARI setzt auch deshalb auf den Werkstoff, weil er exzellente Eigenschaften hat und sich präzise und filigran bearbeiten lässt. Design: Ingmar Boos, Daniel Schulz.

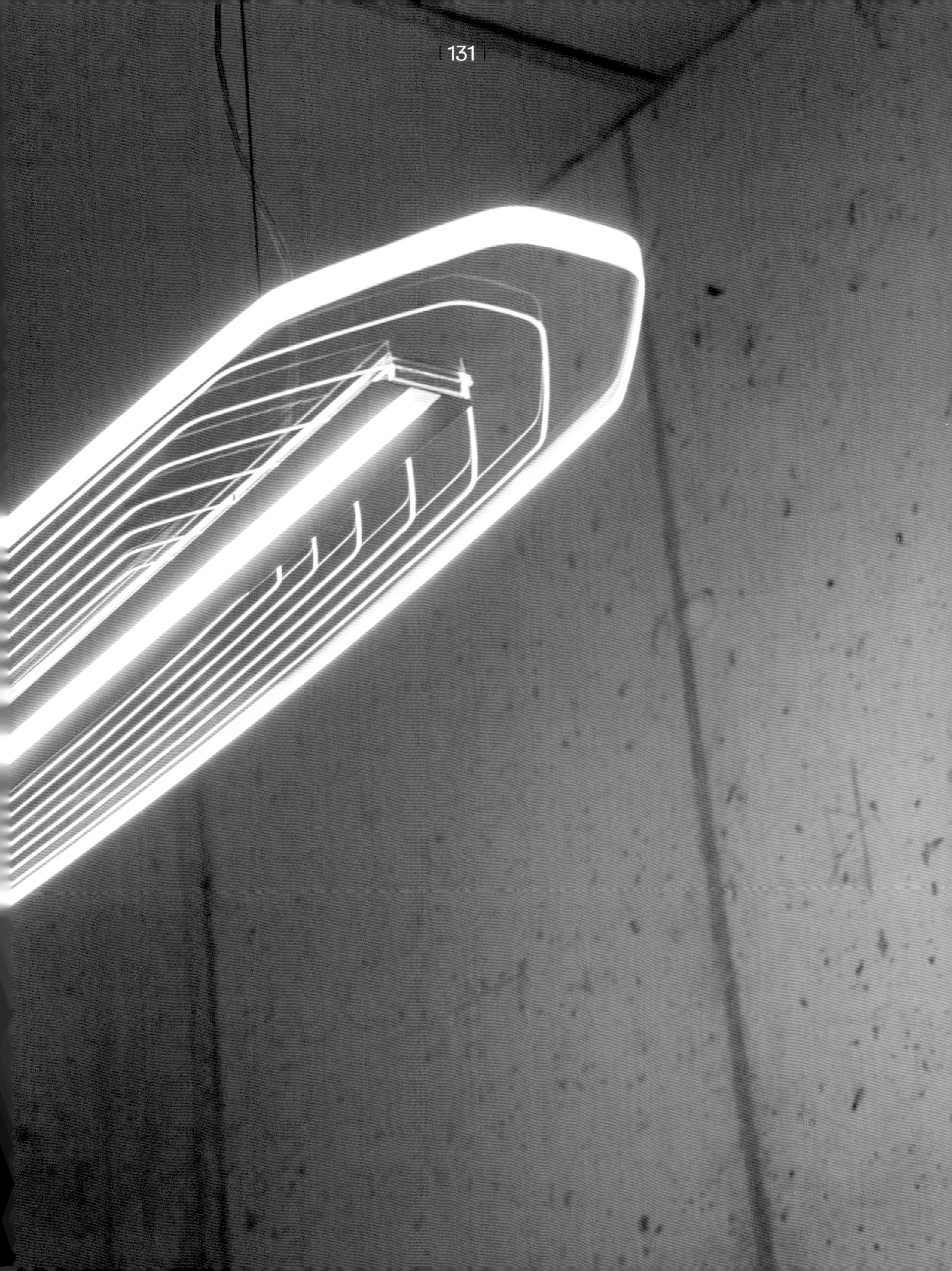

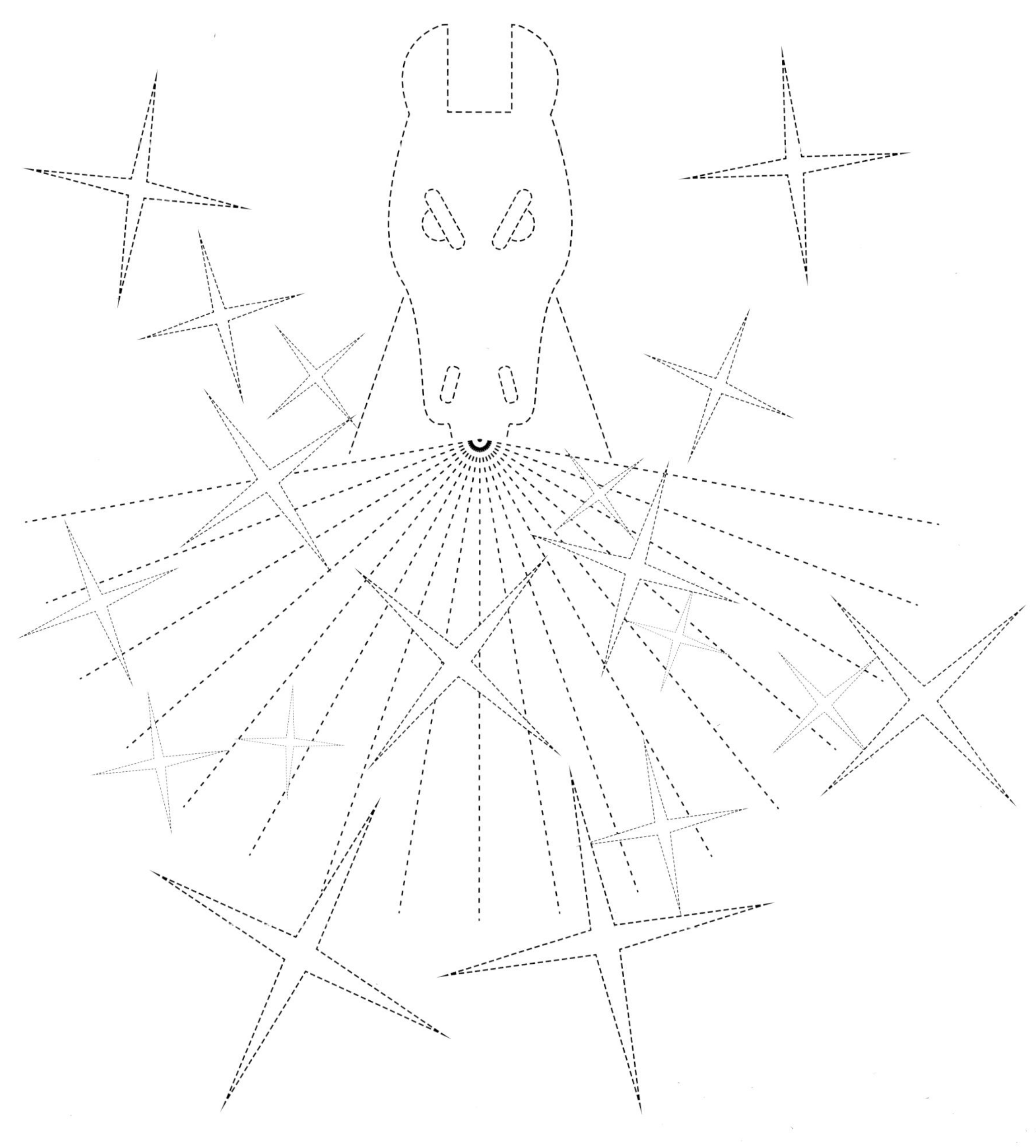

The imagination says,
"I want 170 horses that can
spit light."

PLEXIGLAS® says,
"That's no problem."

Die Fantasie sagt:
„Ich will 170 Pferde, die Licht
spucken können!"

PLEXIGLAS® sagt:
„Geht klar."

Jeep represents feelings of strength, robustness and adventure. A brand maintaining that sort of image needs extremely resilient technology. The light guide for the daytime running light used in the LED headlamps of the Jeep Compass are made from PLEXIMID®, which remains stable, transparent and colorless even under continuous thermal loads.

Jeep steht für das Gefühl von Stärke, Robustheit und Abenteuer. Wer ein solches Image pflegt, bei dem muss auch die Technik unverwüstlich sein. Für die LED-Scheinwerfer des Compass setzt Jeep bei den Lichtleitern für das Tagfahrlicht auf PLEXIMID®, das selbst unter thermischer Dauerbelastung unverändert transparent und farblos bleibt. Design: Jeep Design, Fiat Chrysler Group.

COMPASS

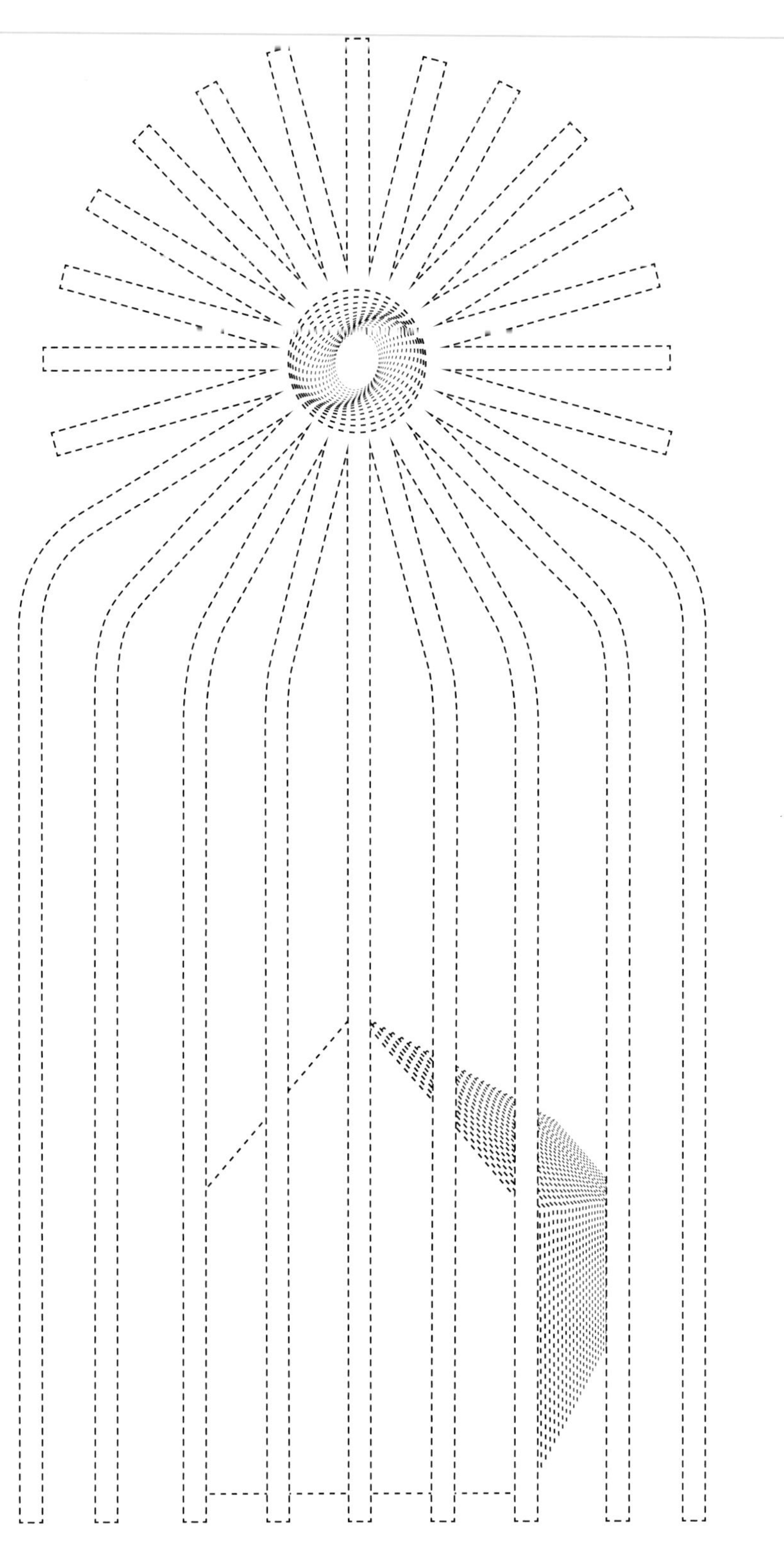

The imagination says,
"I want a villa with curtains
made of light."

PLEXIGLAS® says,
"If that's all."

Die Fantasie sagt:
„Ich will eine Villa mit
Vorhängen aus Licht!"

PLEXIGLAS® sagt:
„Wenn's weiter nichts ist."

Despite its dazzling appearance, the façade of the Victoria's Secret flagship store in Shanghai is not built from tens of thousands of light bars. Victoria's "Secret" behind the optical illusion is quite simple; the seemingly sophisticated 3D effect is produced using grooves of different depths, machined into a total of 104 PLEXIGLAS® panels. The glowing pink is provided by LEDs.

Auch wenn es so wirkt: Die Fassade, die dem Victoria's Secret Flagship Store Shanghai ihren strahlenden Auftritt verschafft, besteht nicht aus Zehntausenden Leuchtstäben. Victoria's „Secret" hinter der optischen Täuschung: Der aufwendig wirkende 3D-Effekt entsteht ganz simpel durch unterschiedlich tiefe Rillen, die in 104 PLEXIGLAS® Platten gefräst wurden. Das strahlende Pink steuern LEDs bei. Design: MBM Construction Wall Engineering.

VICTORIA'S SECRET

FORM FOLLOWS INSPIRATION

PLEXIGLAS® OFFERS SCOPE FOR IDEAS

At the origin of every form, every technical innovation and every art object is an idea. The thoughts of the creator will be mesmerized by this initial concept. For days, sometimes even for weeks or even years. Finally, something emerges from these first thoughts – germinating like a plant from a seed. A product, an object, a piece. In this process, creative minds are dependent on materials that allow them to turn their vision into reality.

PLEXIGLAS® comes to their aid wherever they need to develop something new or improve the existing, as is the case with the "autonomous driving" megatrend. If cars are meant to be guided by computers, that requires many more surround sensors than are usual today. These can either be installed in a visible way or be concealed behind other components that should not however hinder measurements. PLEXIGLAS® already provides suitable solutions for this today.

The vehicle interior will change in light of this megatrend. After all, there will be more time to concentrate on the interior. Where functional elements currently still predominate, the focus in future might lie on an elegant look coupled with ambient lighting and consumer electronics. PLEXIGLAS® provides the scope to pursue these ideas.

PLEXIGLAS® BIETET RAUM FÜR IDEEN

Am Anfang jeder Form, jeder technischen Innovation und jedes Kunstobjekts steht eine Idee. Um diese erste Faszination kreisen die Gedanken des Erschaffers. Tagelang, manchmal Wochen oder gar Jahre. Dann endlich wächst etwas aus diesen ersten Gedanken – wie ein Samenkorn zur Pflanze. Es entsteht ein Produkt, ein Objekt oder ein Gegenstand. Für diesen Prozess sind kreative Köpfe auf Materialien angewiesen, mit denen sie ihre Vision in die Realität umsetzen können.

PLEXIGLAS® ist dort zur Stelle, wo es gilt, Neues zu entwickeln oder Bestehendes zu verbessern. Beispielsweise beim Megatrend „Autonomes Fahren". Denn wenn Fahrzeuge computergesteuert fahren sollen, sind viel mehr Umfeldsensoren notwendig als heute üblich. Diese können sichtbar angebracht werden oder hinter anderen Bauteilen verschwinden, die die Messung aber nicht beeinflussen dürfen. PLEXIGLAS® bietet schon heute dafür passende Varianten an.

Auch der Innenraum von Fahrzeugen wird sich durch den Megatrend verändern, schließlich bleibt mehr Zeit, sich mit dem Interieur auseinanderzusetzen. Wo aktuell noch funktionale Elemente überwiegen, könnte der Fokus künftig auf einer edlen Anmutung gepaart mit stimmungsvoller Beleuchtung und Unterhaltungselektronik liegen – PLEXIGLAS® bietet Raum für diese Ideen.

A sheet of white paper is both a symbol and a metaphor for human culture. It represents a fresh start, order and freedom. With the art installation "Transfer" for the library of the University of Greifswald, Germany, artist Dietrich Förster created an inspiring work using thermoformable translucent PLEXIGLAS® film, reminiscent of flying sheets of paper.

Das weiße Blatt Papier ist Symbol und Metapher der menschlichen Kultur. Es steht für Neubeginn, Ordnung und Freiheit. Der Künstler Dietrich Förster hat mit der Kunstinstallation „Transfer" für die Bibliothek der Ernst-Moritz-Arndt-Universität in Greifswald ein inspirierendes Werk aus thermoplastisch verformbarer, transluzenter PLEXIGLAS® Folie geschaffen, die an fliegende Papierblätter erinnert. Artwork | Kunstwerk: Dietrich Förster.

The Munich Olympic Stadium of 1972 was covered by a tent-like roof designed by the architects firm of Behnisch & Partner and the architect Frei Otto, to resemble the webs of the sheet weaver spider. Inspired by nature, the point-supported, cable-tensioned structure successfully spans large areas. Thanks to the transparent weatherproof PLEXIGLAS® panels, the roof was called "a first taste of heaven" by enthusiastic critics.

Über dem Münchner Olympiastadion von 1972 spannt sich das Zeltdach des Architekturbüros Behnisch & Partner und des Architekten Frei Otto wie die Netze der Baldachinspinne. Inspiriert von der Natur, sollte die punktgestützte, seilverspannte Konstruktion große Spannweiten erreichen. Dank lichtdurchlässiger, witterungsbeständiger PLEXIGLAS® Platten wurde aus dem Dach der „Beginn des Himmels", wie Kritiker schwärmten. Architecture | Architektur: Behnisch & Partner, Frei Otto.

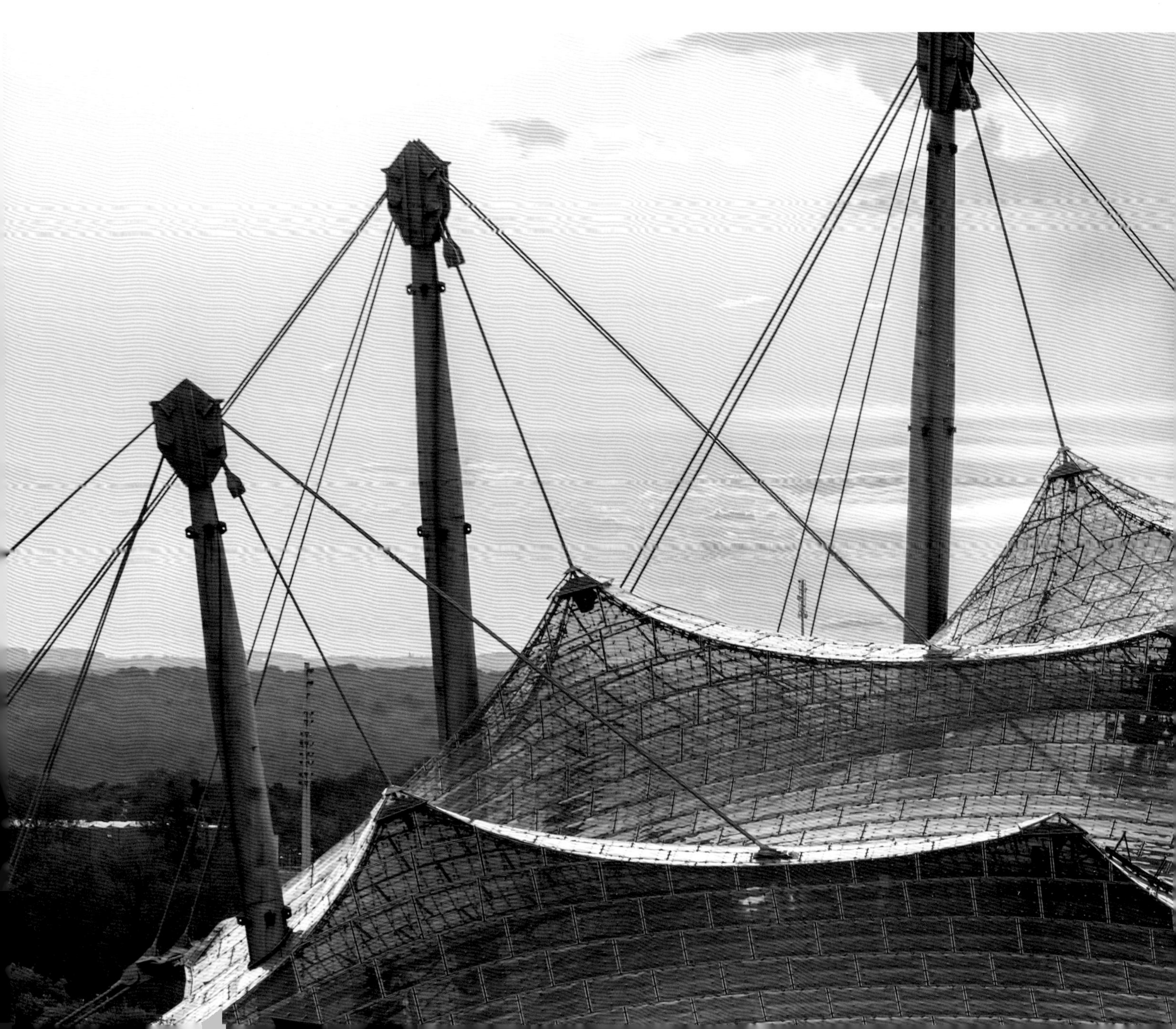

The luminaires by Australian designer Robert Foster penetrate the ground like tusks. Foster called these light-filled shapes "Ossalites" – from the Latin for bone, "os". Controlled by motion sensors, the color of the luminaires oscillates while their LED technology remains concealed. Thermoformed PLEXIGLAS® Satinice, six millimeters thick, ensures homogeneous light distribution.

Die Leuchten des australischen Designers Robert Foster durchbohren wie Stoßzähne den Boden. Foster taufte die Lichtobjekte daher „Ossalites" – vom lateinischen „Os" für Knochen. Gesteuert durch Bewegungsmelder oszilliert die Farbe der Leuchten, deren LED-Technik unsichtbar bleibt. Thermisch geformtes, sechs Millimeter dünnes PLEXIGLAS® Satinice sorgt dabei für eine gleichmäßige Lichtstreuung. Design: Robert Foster.

Delicate, leaf-like PLEXIGLAS® elements give the Artemide Chlorophilia 2 luminaire flowing, wave-like and structured surfaces, generating an interplay of light and shadow. The centrally suspended light fixture emits indirect light, which is broken up over two levels by radially arranged elements, whose form and structure are reminiscent of the foliage of trees.

Zarte, blattähnliche Elemente aus PLEXIGLAS® geben der Artemide-Leuchte Chlorophilia 2 fließende, wellenförmige und strukturierte Oberflächen und erzeugen ein Spiel aus Licht und Schatten. Der zentral abgehängte, glänzende Leuchtkörper emittiert indirektes Licht, das auf zwei Ebenen durch radial angeordnete Elemente gebrochen wird, die in Form und Struktur an das Blattwerk von Bäumen erinnern. Design: Ross Lovegrove.

The Ameluna pendant luminaire combines the illumination expertise of Artemide with the philosophy of sensual clarity at Mercedes-Benz Style, telling a story that goes beyond the design object itself. The starting point is the fascination with deep ocean lifeforms that are capable of generating light. The resultant lighting phenomena became a central inspiration for this development from Ameluna.

Die Pendelleuchte Ameluna verbindet die Lichtkompetenz von Artemide mit der Philosophie der sinnlichen Klarheit von Mercedes-Benz Style und erzählt eine Geschichte, die über das Designobjekt hinausgeht. Am Anfang stand die Faszination für Lebewesen der Tiefsee, die die Fähigkeit besitzen, Licht zu erzeugen. Die dabei entstehenden Lichtphänomene waren eine zentrale Inspiration zur Entwicklung von Ameluna. Design: Artemide & Mercedes-Benz Style.

The light concept of the Ameluna pendant luminaire is based on an optoelectronic innovation, which is integrated into a transparent PLEXIGLAS® light fixture. The outline of the luminaire is a circle, while the surrounding body is characterized by a form in a state of dynamic tension. Suspended on super-thin support wires, the luminaire appears to float freely in mid-air.

Das Lichtkonzept der Pendelleuchte Ameluna basiert auf einer optoelektronischen Innovation, die in einen transparenten Leuchtenkörper aus PLEXIGLAS® integriert ist. Ein Kreis bildet den Grundriss der Leuchte, während der Korpus durch eine dynamisch gespannte Form geprägt ist. Aufgehängt an hauchdünnen Trägerseilen, scheint die Leuchte frei im Raum zu schweben.

Design: Artemide & Mercedes-Benz Style.

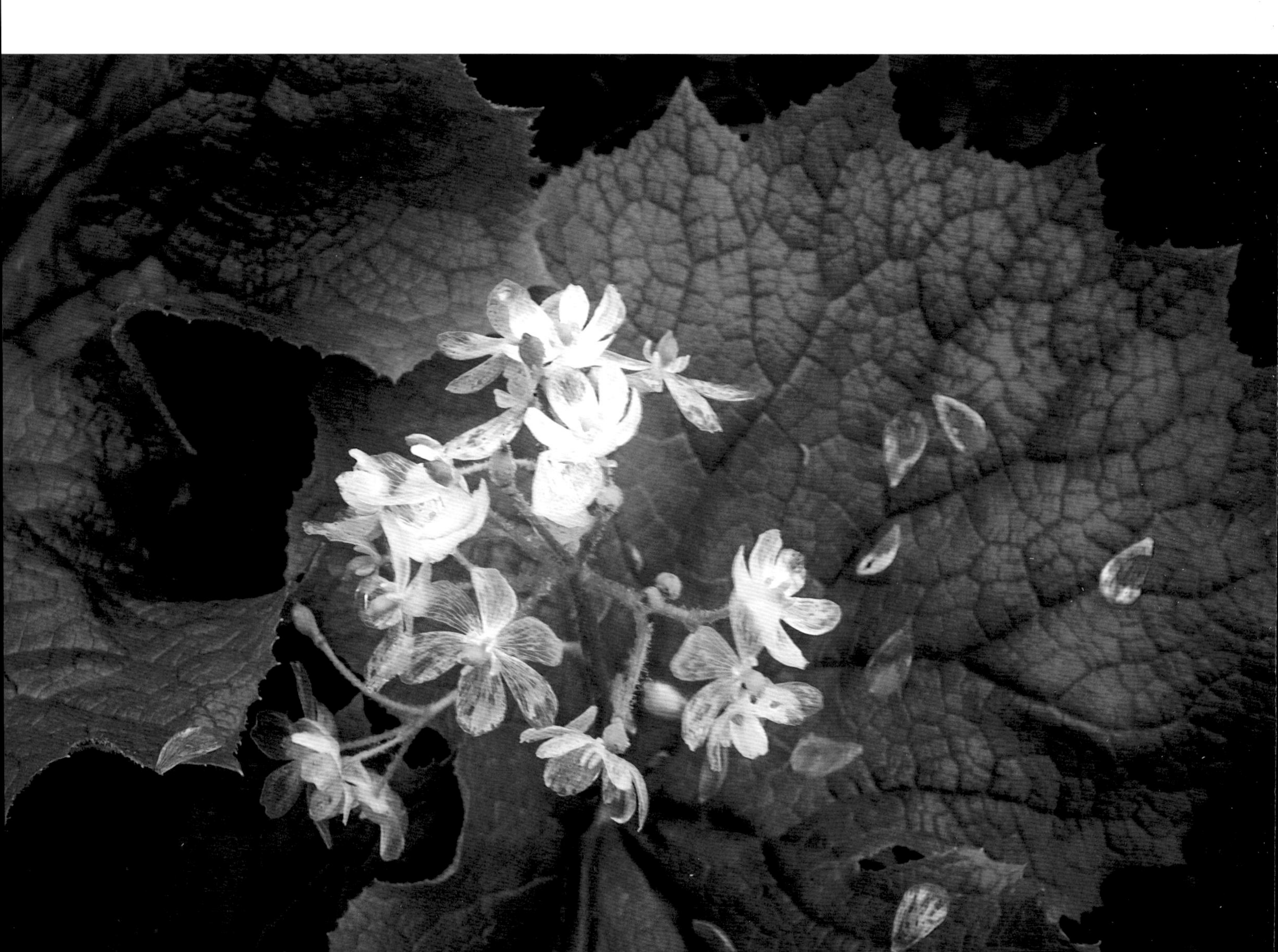

The design of the Diphy luminaire is inspired by the Diphylleia grayi flower whose white petals become transparent on contact with water. In contrast to nature, a diffuser made of transparent PLEXIGLAS® ensures that the luminaire becomes almost invisible when it is switched off. When it is turned on, the laser-incised micro engravings in the diffuser provide for even, dazzle-free distribution of the LED light.

Die Gestaltung der Leuchte Diphy ist durch die Blütenpflanze Diphylleya Grayi inspiriert, deren weiße Blütenblätter transparent werden, sobald sie mit Wasser in Berührung kommen. Im Unterschied zur Natur sorgt ein Lichtleiter aus transparentem PLEXIGLAS® dafür, dass die ausgeschaltete Leuchte nahezu unsichtbar bleibt. Eingeschaltet erzeugt die Laser-Mikrogravur im Lichtleiter eine gleichmäßige, blendfreie Verteilung des LED-Lichts. Design: Linea Light Group.

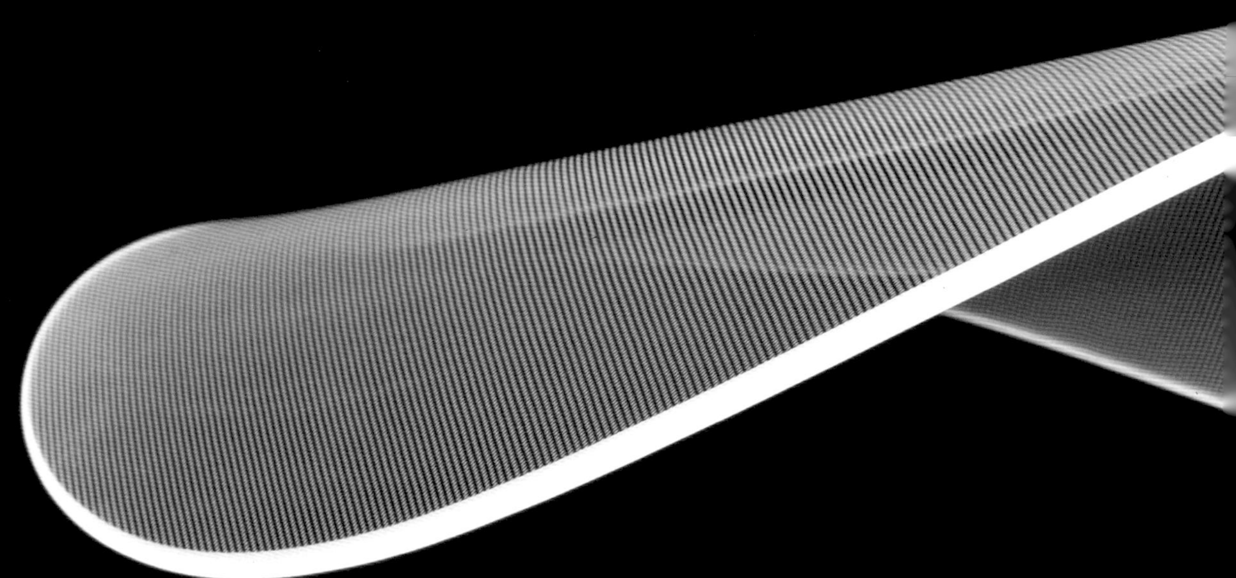

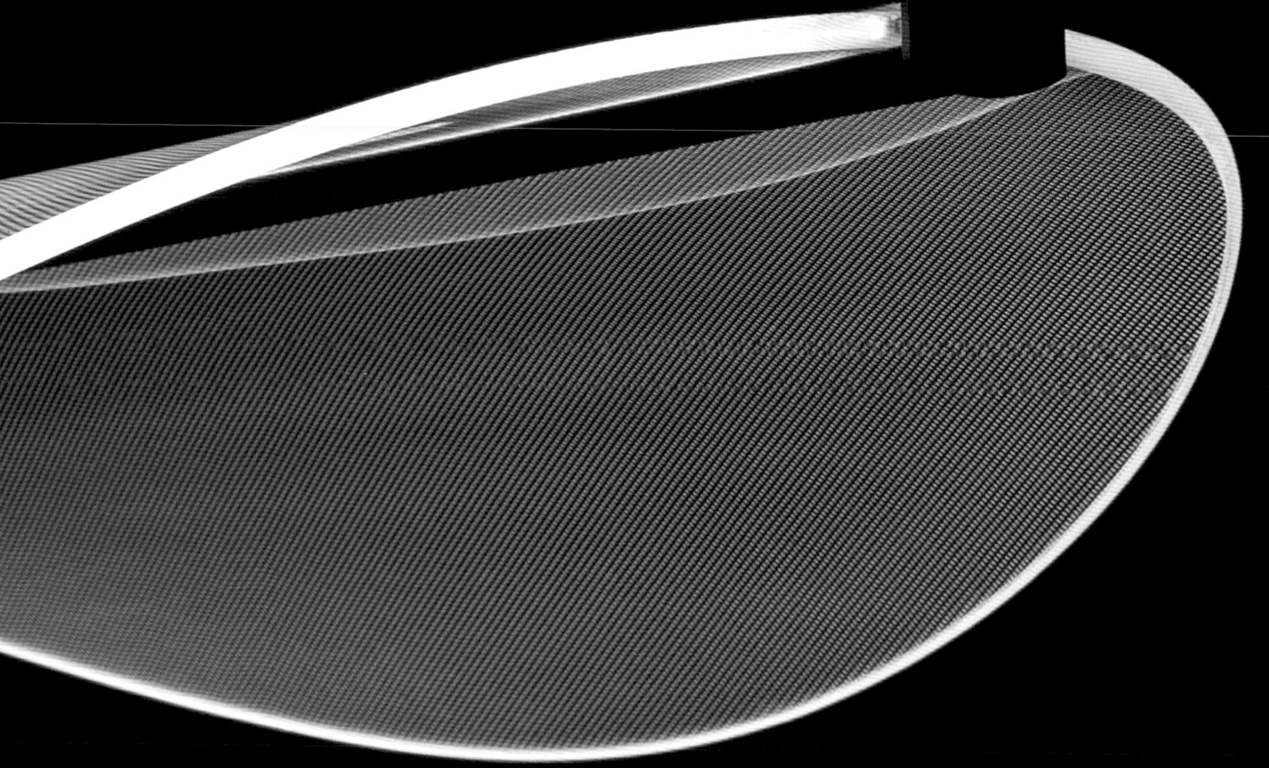

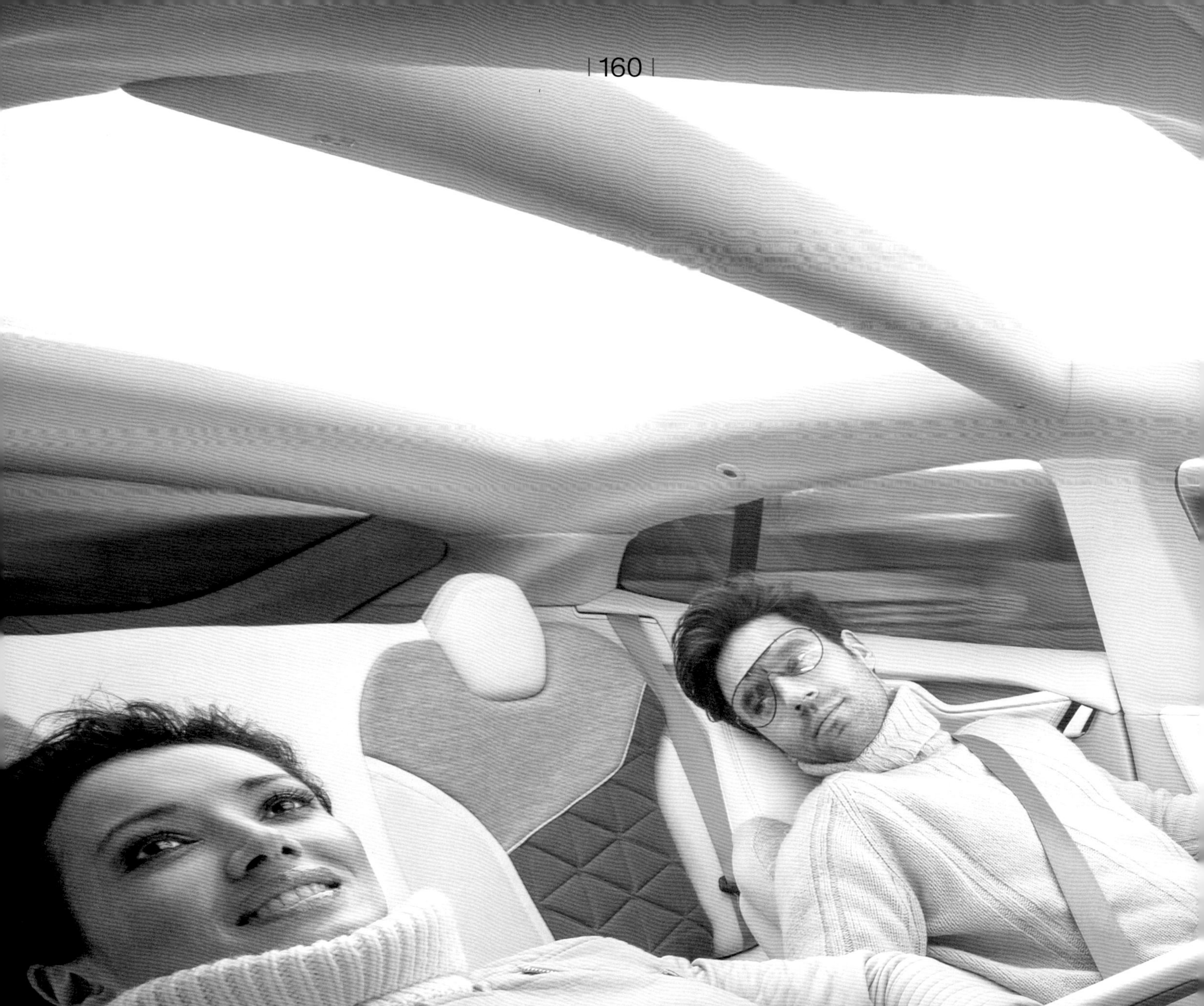

Electric powertrains, autonomous driving and networked vehicles: the automotive industry is undergoing a profound process of transfor mation. The "Xchange" study from the Swiss think tank Rinspeed delivers some insights into the future of autonomous driving. Also on board is PLEXIGLAS®. Not just for display applications in the vehicle interior – the revolutionary panoramic roof made from acrylic glass gives an inspiring view of the future.

Elektrische Antriebe, autonomes Fahren und vernetzte Fahrzeuge: Die Automobilindustrie erfährt einen grundsätzlichen Wandel. Mit der Studie „Xchange" gibt die Schweizer Ideenschmiede Rinspeed einen Einblick in die Zukunft des autonomen Fahrens. Mit an Bord: PLEXIGLAS®. Nicht nur für Displayanwendungen im Innenraum – auch das revolutionäre Panoramadach aus dem Acrylglas gibt einen inspirierenden Ausblick in die Zukunft. Design: Rinspeed, Frank M. Rinderknecht.

Eberspächer

HARMAN
HAPPY
Pharell Williams, Happy
Media Center
Phone
Navigation
Settings
Driver Assist
Apps
SmartConnect

18:46
Mittwoch, 5. Februar

The SUV concept car "ID. ROOMZZ" by Volkswagen is breaking new ground with its interior. Intelligent systems control the model autonomously. Passengers are provided with information via interactive light zones, and are able to adjust a wide range of configurations. PLEXIGLAS® supports the passengers with an infotainment module, an illuminated steering wheel, lighting strips along the bases of the windows, and a continuous display with information about the surrounding area.

Die SUV-Studie „ID. ROOMZZ" von Volkswagen beschreitet im Interieur neue Wege. Intelligente Systeme bewegen das Modell autonom. Insassen werden dabei durch interaktive Lichtzonen mit Informationen versorgt und können umfangreiche Konfigurationen vornehmen. PLEXIGLAS® unterstützt die Insassen mit einem Infotainment-Modul, einem beleuchteten Lenkrad, Lichtbändern an den Scheibenwurzeln sowie einem Laufband mit Informationen über die Umgebung. Design: Volkswagen.

IQ.LIGHT

With electrifying ease, the SUV concept car "ID. ROOMZZ" from Volkswagen cruises into the future, silent and emission-free. The seemingly monolithic exterior emphasizes that PLEXIGLAS® is likewise living up to its reputation as an inspirational material. The fascinating qualities of the material are expressed in the headlamps, the luminescent emblems and door handles, the roof console inserts, and the light signatures at the rear.

Mit elektrischer Leichtigkeit bewegt sich die SUV-Studie „ID. ROOMZZ“ von Volkswagen geräuschlos und emissionsfrei in Richtung Zukunft. Das monolithisch wirkende Exterieur unterstreicht, dass auch PLEXIGLAS® seinem Anspruch als inspirierender Werkstoff gerecht wird. Die Faszination des Materials kommt in den Scheinwerfern, den leuchtenden Emblemen und Türgriffen, den Dachkonsoleneinlegern und den Lichtsignaturen am Heck zum Ausdruck. Design: Volkswagen.

A8 L
IN A 8501
D

The innovative rear lights of the Audi A8 extend across the entire width of the vehicle rear. With the help of PLEXIGLAS®, the three modules create a clearly visible band of light, emphasizing the luxurious presence of this top-end model. Because the light elements are controlled by segments, this permits a new form of design: with inspirational light orchestration and dynamic motion of the indicators.

Die innovativen Rückleuchten des Audi A8 erstrecken sich über die gesamte Breite des Fahrzeughecks. Mithilfe von PLEXIGLAS® erzeugen die drei Module ein deutlich wahrnehmbares Lichtband und betonen die luxuriöse Präsenz des Premiummodells. Da die Lichtelemente segmentweise angesteuert werden, erlauben sie eine neue Form der Gestaltung: mit inspirierender Lichtinszenierung und dynamischem Verlauf des Blinklichts. Design: AUDI.

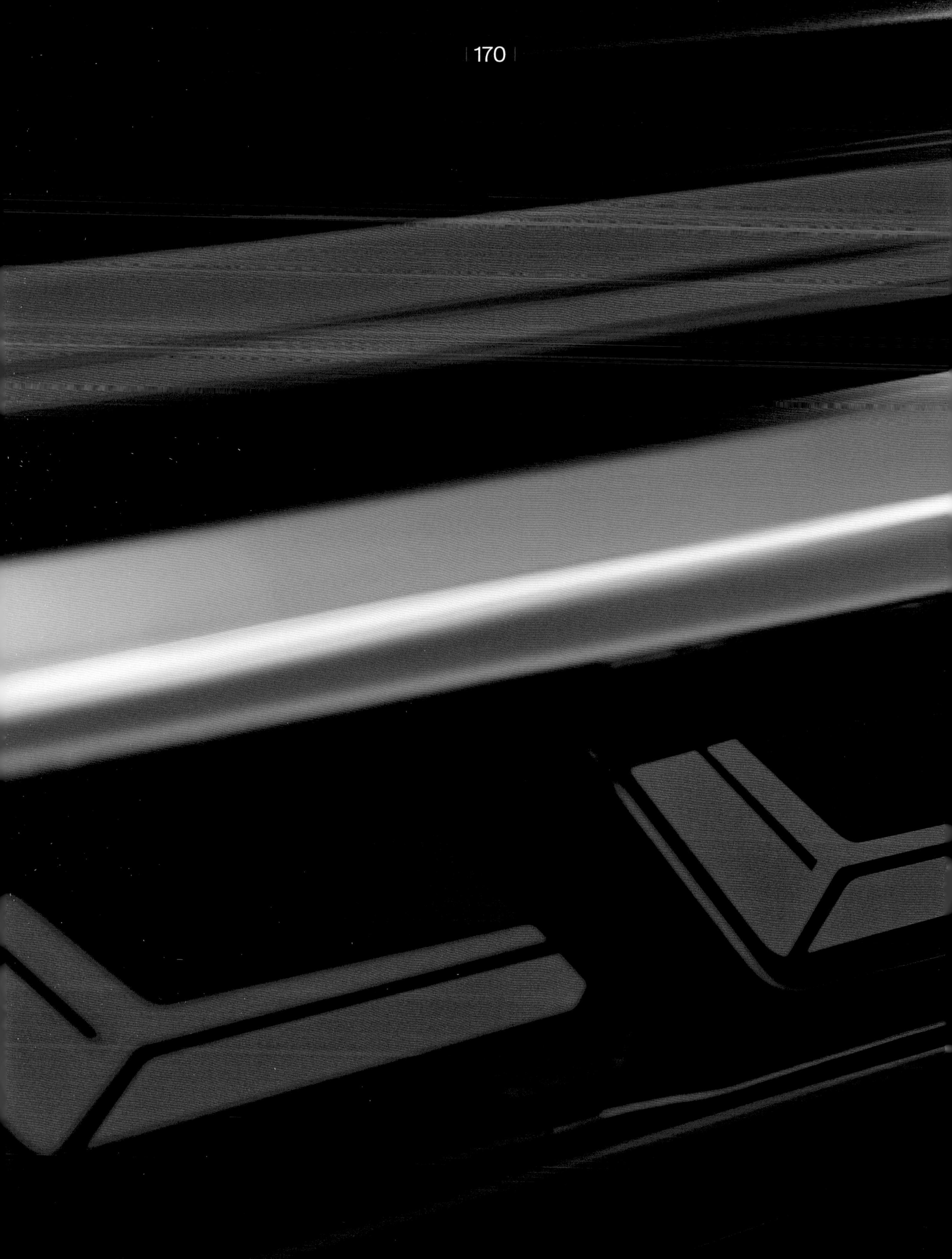

EQC 400
4MATIC
S EQ 114E

The Mercedes-Benz EQC is the embodiment of progressive luxury. The electric powertrain ensures virtually silent, emission-free driving. The new aesthetic radiates calm and modernity. The striking LED back light bar of the vehicle creates a fascinating eye-catcher, a visual exclamation mark particularly at night, capturing its surroundings at literally the speed of light with its signal red PLEXIGLAS®.

Der Mercedes-Benz EQC verkörpert progressiven Luxus. Der elektrische Antrieb sorgt für nahezu lautloses, emissionsfreies Fahren. Die neue Ästhetik strahlt Ruhe und Modernität aus. Einen faszinierenden Blickfang bieten die markanten LED-Lichtbander am Heck, die vor allem nachts Ausrufezeichen setzen und dank signalrotem PLEXIGLAS® ihre Umgebung förmlich in Lichtgeschwindigkeit für sich einnehmen. Design: Mercedes-Benz.

PORSCHE
S GO 6213

The new characteristic taillight strip across the rear of the Porsche Macan is like a striking bold line, underscoring the powerful design. The visual effect is reinforced by the lateral function lights. The taillight strip is constructed from four different PLEXIGLAS® molding compound types, and has a sculptured surface structure that produces inspiring effects in combination with an intelligent lighting control system.

Wie ein markanter Strich betont das neue charakteristische Lichtband des Porsche Macan das kraftvoll gestaltete Heck. Optisch ergänzt wird es durch die seitlichen Funktionsleuchten. Das Lichtband, aufgebaut aus vier verschiedenen PLEXIGLAS® Formmassen, besitzt eine skulpturartige Oberflächenstruktur, die in Verbindung mit einer intelligenten Lichtsteuerung inspirierende Effekte erzielt. Design: Porsche.

FORM FOLLOWS RESPONSIBILITY

PLEXIGLAS® IS SUSTAINABLE

Plastics are not all the same. Today, there is a suitable material for every application area. Take PLEXIGLAS® for instance, which comes into play whenever long-lasting end products are required: vehicle components, façades, roofing, lighting – all generally not short-lived disposable products. Sometimes they even stay in use for decades. In that regard, the material contributes to the sustainable use of resources.

Would you like an example? The manufacturer offers a 30-year guarantee against yellowing on all colorless PLEXIGLAS® sheets. That means, while other transparent plastic sheets need to be replaced twice after initial fitting in this time period, the trademarked PMMA remains virtually unaltered. Nothing changes – and no ingredients separate out either. The product is free of hormone-like substances (e.g. BPA) and heavy metals. It contains neither asbestos nor formaldehyde, CFCs, PCB, PCT nor plasticizers.

In addition to its durability, PLEXIGLAS® is also notable for its recycling properties. Once the material does eventually reach the end of its useful life, it can be fully recycled either by being broken down into its original chemical constituents or through simple, direct repurposing in thermoplastic processes.

This makes PLEXIGLAS® a future proof alternative to many other plastics – and it also contributes to making applications more sustainable. Thanks to this invention, cars and airplanes are lighter and therefore more fuel-efficient, supermarkets and sports arenas can be lit more energy efficiently, greenhouses are operated in a more climate-friendly way, and façades and window frames are more durable.

PLEXIGLAS® IST NACHHALTIG

Kunststoff ist nicht gleich Kunststoff. Für jedes Anwendungsgebiet gibt es heutzutage das passende Material. So wie PLEXIGLAS®, das häufig dann ins Spiel kommt, wenn langlebige Endprodukte gefragt sind: Bauteile für Fahrzeuge, Fassaden, Überdachungen, Leuchten – alles im Normalfall keine schnelllebigen Wegwerfprodukte. Manchmal verbleiben sie sogar für Jahrzehnte in der Anwendung. Der Werkstoff trägt damit zu einem nachhaltigen Umgang mit Ressourcen bei.

Beispiel gefällig? Für nahezu alle farblosen PLEXIGLAS® Platten garantiert der Hersteller 30 Jahre Vergilbungsfreiheit. Das heißt: Während andere transparente Kunststoffplatten in diesem Zeitraum nach dem Originaleinbau bereits zweimal ausgetauscht wurden, ist das Marken-PMMA noch immer nahezu unverändert. Es verändert sich nicht – und es sondert auch keine Inhaltsstoffe ab: so ist es beispielsweise frei von hormonähnlichen Stoffen (z. B. BPA) und Schwermetallen. Es enthält weder Asbest noch Formaldehyd, FCKW, PCB und PCT oder zum Beispiel Weichmacher.

Neben der Langlebigkeit überzeugt PLEXIGLAS® auch durch seine Recyclingfähigkeit: Denn wenn das Material irgendwann doch am Ende seiner Nutzungsdauer angekommen ist, kann es vollständig recycelt werden. Entweder durch chemische Rückspaltung in die Ausgangsstoffe oder indem es einfach direkt in thermoplastischen Verfahren wiederverwendet wird.

Der Werkstoff ist damit eine zukunftstaugliche Alternative zu vielen anderen Kunststoffen – und es leistet einen Beitrag dazu, dass Anwendungen nachhaltiger werden. Dank PLEXIGLAS® werden Autos und Flugzeuge leichter und somit kraftstoffsparender, Supermärkte und Sportarenen energieeffizient beleuchtet, Gewächshäuser klimaschonend betrieben und Fassaden und Fenster langlebig.

Supermarkets have high energy requirements. The third biggest consumer of energy is the permanent lighting. However, the TECTON strip light system from Zumtobel consumes 40 percent less energy than fluorescent tube lights. Part of the energy-saving program consists of PLEXIGLAS® covers with lens optics, providing high-efficiency delivery of the LED light to where it is really needed: lots on the shelves, less on the floor.

Der Energiebedarf von Supermärkten ist groß. Drittgrößter Energiefresser: das Dauerlicht. Doch das Lichtbandsystem TECTON von Zumtobel verbraucht im Vergleich zu Leuchtstoffröhren 40 Prozent weniger Energie. Teil des Sparprogramms sind Abdeckungen aus PLEXIGLAS® mit Linsenoptiken, die das LED-Licht hocheffizient dorthin lenken, wo es wirklich gebraucht wird: viel im Regal, wenig auf dem Boden. Design: Zumtobel.

Temperature management in greenhouses consumes a lot of energy. The manufacturer Technokas came up with the idea of a roof that uses "excess" solar energy, but allows through enough diffuse light for the plants. The solution is to use injection-molded PLEXIGLAS® Fresnel lenses, which concentrate the sunlight onto a collector. The energy gathered in this way provides heating at night, and absorption cooling when temperatures get too high.

Das Temperaturmanagement in Gewächshäusern braucht viel Energie. Die Idee des Herstellers Technokas: ein Dach, das „überschüssige" Sonnenenergie nutzt, aber ausreichend diffuses Licht für die Pflanzen durchlässt. Die Lösung: spritzgegossene Fresnellinsen aus PLEXIGLAS®, die das Sonnenlicht auf einen Kollektor konzentrieren. Die so gewonnene Energie sorgt bei Nacht für Wärme und bei Hitze für Absorptionskühlung.

Architecture | Architektur: Technokas.

PHOTO AND IMAGE CREDITS

Photo and image credits | Foto- und Bildnachweise

Design icons made of plastic

PF – Phenol formaldehyde resins (Phenoplastics)

Baby Brownie, 1934
Manufacturer: Eastman Kodak Company, USA
Design: Walter Dorwin Teague
Photo: Die Neue Sammlung – The Design Museum, Munich, Germany
Photographer: Angela Bröhan, Munich and Berlin, Germany

Purma Spezial, 1937
Manufacturer: Thomas De La Rue, UK
Purma Cameras, UK
Design: Raymond Loewy
Photo: Die Neue Sammlung – The Design Museum, Munich, Germany
Photographer: Alexander Laurenzo, Munich, Germany

Radio Nurse, 1937
Manufacturer: Zenith Radio Corporation, USA
Design: Isamu Noguchi
Photo: Die Neue Sammlung – The Design Museum, Munich, Germany
Photographer: Alexander Laurenzo, Munich, Germany

Philishave, Type 7730, 1939
Manufacturer: Royal Philips, The Netherlands
Design: Alexandre Horowitz
Photo: Royal Philips N.V. & Philips Company Archives, Eindhoven, The Netherlands

Ducati Microphone, 1940
Manufacturer: Ducati, Italy
Design: Gio Ponti
Photo: Die Neue Sammlung – The Design Museum, Munich, Germany
Photographer: Alexander Laurenzo, Munich, Germany

Braun sixtant SM 31, 1962
Manufacturer: Braun, Germany
Design: Hans Gugelot, Gerd Alfred Müller
Photo: Braun P&G, Förderkreis Braun Sammlung e.V., Kronberg, Germany

---

PUR – Polyurethane

Egg, 1958
Manufacturer: Fritz Hansen, Denmark
Design: Arne Jacobsen
Photo: Fritz Hansen, Allerød, Denmark

Malitte, 1966
Manufacturer: Gavina, Italy
Design: Roberto Sebastian Matta
Photo: Die Neue Sammlung – The Design Museum, Munich, Germany
Photographer: Angela Bröhan, Munich and Berlin, Germany

Garden Egg, 1968
Manufacturer: Elastogran, Germany
Design: Peter Ghyczy
Photo: Pamono.de, Berlin, Germany

Cactus, 1971
Manufacturer: Gufram, Italy
Design: Guido Drocco, Franco Mello
Photo: Die Neue Sammlung –
The Design Museum, Munich, Germany
Photographer: Alexander Laurenzo,
Munich, Germany

Clover, 2011
Manufacturer: Kundalini, Italy
Design: Brodie Neill
Photo: Kundalini, Trezzano sul Naviglio,
Milan, Italy

PC – Polycarbonate

Lamy 2000, 1966
Manufacturer: C. Josef Lamy, Germany
Design: Hans Gugelot, Gerd Alfred Müller
Photo: C. Josef Lamy, Heidelberg,
Germany

iMac 1998
Manufacturer: Apple, USA
Design: Jonathan Ive, Apple Industrial
Design Team
Photo: Apple, Cupertino, USA

Rimowa Salsa, 2000
Manufacturer: Rimowa, Germany
Design: In-house Design
Photo: Rimowa, Cologne, Germany

Abyss, 2006
Manufacturer: Kundalini, Italy
Design: Osko+Deichmann
Photo: Kundalini, Trezzano sul Naviglio,
Milan, Italy

Printable Eco Bottle, 2016
Manufacturer: Tupperware, Aalst, Belgium
Design: Tupperware Worldwide
Product Development Team
Photo: Tupperware General Services,
Aalst, Belgium

UP – Unsaturated polyester

La Chaise, 1948
Manufacturer: Vitra, Switzerland
Design: Charles & Ray Eames
Copyright: Eames Office, California, USA
Photo: Vitra Design Museum, Weil am
Rhein, Germany
Photographer: Jürgen Hans,
objektfotograf.ch, Zurich, Switzerland

No. 151 / Tulip Chair, 1956
Manufacurer: Knoll International, USA
Design: Eero Saarinen
Photo: Die Neue Sammlung –
The Design Museum, Munich, Germany
Photographer: Alexander Laurenzo,
Munich, Germany

BA 1171 / Bofinger Chair, 1964
Manufacturer: Menzolit-Werke Albert
Schmidt for Wilhelm Bofinger,
Germany
Design: Helmut Bätzner
Copyright: Bofinger Produktion / Baresel-
Bofinger, Heilbronn, Germany
Photo: Quittenbaum Kunstauktionen,
Munich, Germany

Pastilli, 1967
Design: Eero Aarnio
Copyright: Eero Aarnio Archives, Finland
Photo: Quittenbaum Kunstauktionen,
Munich, Germany

Tomato, 1971
Design: Eero Aarnio
Copyright: Eero Aarnio Archives, Finland
Ownership: Die Neue Sammlung –
The Design Museum, Munich, Germany
Photo: Adelta, Helsinki, Finland

T.S. Speedy Chef, 2008
Manufacturer: Tupperware, Aalst, Belgium
Design: Tupperware Worldwide
Product Development Team
Photo: Tupperware General Services,
Aalst, Belgium

ABS – Acrylonitrile butadiene styrene

Radio Cube TS 502, 1964
Manufacturer: Brionvega, Italy
Design: Marco Zanuso, Richard Sapper
Photo: Quittenbaum Kunstauktionen,
Munich, Germany

Toot-a-Loop,
Panasonic Radio R-72 S, 1969
Manufacturer: Matsushita, Japan
Design: unknown
Photo: Die Neue Sammlung –
The Design Museum, Munich, Germany
Photographer: Angela Bröhan, Munich
and Berlin, Germany

Nivico TV, Model 3240 GM, 1970
Manufacturer: JVC, Japan
Design: unknown
Photo: Die Neue Sammlung –
The Design Museum, Munich, Germany
Photographer: Alexander Laurenzo,
Munich, Germany

PHOTO AND IMAGE CREDITS

Weltron 2005, 1970
Manufacturer: Weltron, Japan
Design: unknown
Photo: Die Neue Sammlung –
The Design Museum, Munich, Germany
Photographer: Angela Bröhan, Munich
and Berlin, Germany

Air Multiplier™, 2009
Manufacturer: Dyson, UK
Design: James Dyson
Photo: Dyson, Malmesbury, UK

Drop, 1958/2014
Manufacturer: Fritz Hansen, Denmark
Design: Arne Jacobsen
Photo: Fritz Hansen, Allerød, Denmark

PMMA – Polymethyl methacrylate

VB 101 w/PLEXIGLAS® Chair, 1954
Manufacturer: Vitra, Switzerland
Design: Hans Theodor Baumann, 1952/53
Copyright: Luise Lenz, née Baumann,
Schopfheim, Germany
Photo: Vitra Design Museum, Weil
am Rhein, Germany
Photographer: Jürgen Hans,
objektfotograf.ch, Zurich, Switzerland

Braun SK 4, 1956
Photo: Braun SK 6, 1960/SK 61, 1961
Manufacturer: Braun, Germany
Design: Hans Gugelot, Dieter Rams
Photographer: Heinz Hefele, Darmstadt,
Germany

Champagne Chair, 1957
Manufacturer: Formes Nouvelles,
Rennes, France
Design: Estelle Laverne, Erwine Laverne
Photo: Quittenbaum Kunstauktionen,
Munich, Germany

Gherpe Lamp, 1967
Manufacturer: Poltronova, Italy
Design: Superstudio
Photo: Quittenbaum Kunstauktionen,
Munich, Germany

Bubble Chair, 1968
Design: Eero Aarnio
Copyright: Eero Aarnio Archives, Finland
Photo: Quittenbaum Kunstauktionen,
Munich, Germany

Black ST 201, 1969
Manufacturer: Brionvega, Italy
Design: Marco Zanuso, Richard Sapper
Photo: Red Dot, Essen, Germany
Photographer: Marco Wydmuch,
Gelsenkirchen, Germany

Basic, 1991
Manufacturer: Alfi, Germany
Design: Ross Lovegrove, Julian Brown
Photo: Alfi, Wertheim, Germany

Chapter | Kapitel
Form follows experience

Table lamp, 1957
Photographer: Heinz Hefele, Darmstadt,
Germany

Ocari Stelaro, 2017
bsd - Boos & Schulz Designagentur,
Ginsheim-Gustavsburg, Germany

MINI, 1959, 2000
BMW Group, Munich, Germany

VP Globe, 1969
Verpan, Horsens, Denmark

Ameluna, 2016
Artemide, Pregnana Milanese, Italy

VW Käfer, 1950
Adobe Stock, stock.adobe.com
Photographer: Martin Debus

Audi Q5, 2016
AUDI AG, Ingolstadt, Germany

Olympic Stadium Munich, 1972
Getty Images International, Ireland
Photographer: Peter von Felbert / LOOK-foto

Allianz Arena, Munich, 2005
Getty Images International, Ireland
Photographer: Thomas Streubel / LOOK-foto

Chapter | Kapitel
Form follows performance

WWK Arena, 2017
Bernhard & Kögl Architekten, Augsburg, Germany
Photographer: Jens Weber, Munich, Germany

Godswill Akpabio International Stadium, 2014
Julius Berger International, Wiesbaden, Germany

Trilux Lateralo Ring LED, 2015
Trilux, Arnsberg, Germany

Transparency LED, 2014
Schmitz | Wila, Schmitz-Leuchten, Arnsberg, Germany

Maul LED desk luminaire, 2016
Jakob Maul, Bad König-Zell, Germany

Thermomix TM5, 2014
Vorwerk, Wuppertal, Germany

Touchpad Mercedes-Benz S-Class Coupé, 2014
Daimler AG, Stuttgart, Germany

Opel Crossland X, 2017
Opel Automobile, Rüsselsheim, Germany

BMW 5 series rear lights, 2017
BMW Group, Munich, Germany

MINI Union Jack LED rear lights, 2018
BMW Group, Munich, Germany

Chapter | Kapitel
Form follows reliability

Floodlight 20 LED
Siteco, Traunreut, Germany

Audi A6 allroad quattro, 2014
AUDI AG, Ingolstadt, Germany

MINI Clubman, 2015
BMW Group, Munich, Germany

Volkswagen Touareg
Volkswagen AG, Wolfsburg, Germany

Volkswagen T-Roc, 2017
Volkswagen AG, Wolfsburg, Germany

Opel Insignia Grand Sport, 2017
Opel Automobile, Rüsselsheim, Germany

Reiss Store London, 2008
Photographer: Will Pryce, London, UK

Raiffeisen Regionalbank Hall in Tirol
Photo: Raiffeisen Regionalbank Hall in Tirol, Austria

Kunsthaus Graz, 2003
Universalmuseum Joanneum, Graz, Austria
Photographer: Christian Plach

Gealan acrylcolor, Irish Bank, Dublin, Ireland
Gealan Fenster-Systeme, Oberkotzau, Germany

Split & Store, 2016
RENS, Eindhoven, The Netherlands
Photographer: Aisha Zeijpveld

Chapter | Kapitel
Form follows emotion

Hotel Clarion, Helsinki, Finland, 2016
Berndorf Bäderbau, www.berndorf-baederbau.com, Berndorf, Austria

Table lamps "Escargot2" THL 02 & "La perle" THL 01, 2002
Tecnolumen, Bremen, Germany

Pendant lamps "Mon coeur" HHL 03 & "Escargot2" HHL 02
Tecnolumen, Bremen, Germany

Kundalini Shakti, 2001
Kundalini, Trezzano sul Naviglio, Milan, Italy

Mercedes-Benz C-Class Coupé, 2015
Daimler AG, Stuttgart, Germany

Lounge Chair lumiluxE
Axis, Nuremberg, Germany
Photographer: Burkhard Jacob

Ocari Liviano, 2016
bsd - Boos & Schulz Designagentur, Ginsheim-Gustavsburg, Germany

Jeep Compass Night Eagle, 2019
FCA Germany AG, Fiat Chrysler Automobiles, Frankfurt, Germany

Victoria's Secret Store, Shanghai, China
Photo: Evonik Performance Materials, Essen, Germany

PHOTO AND IMAGE CREDITS

Chapter | Kapitel
Form follows inspiration

Stack of paper
Adobe Stock, stock.adobe.com
Photographer: Andreas Mueller

Transfer art installation, 2003
Ernst-Moritz-Arndt University of Greifswald, Germany
Copyright: Dietrich Förster

Spider web
Adobe Stock, stock.adobe.com
Photographer: TSpider

Olympic Stadium Munich, 1972
Getty Images International, Ireland
Photo: Westend61

Big ivory tusks
Adobe Stock, stock.adobe.com
Photographer: boyzzzzz

Ossalites installation
Robert Foster, F!NK + Co, Canberra, Australia
Photo: DMC Photography

Branch of pumpkin leaves
Adobe Stock, stock.adobe.com
Photographer: boonchuay1970

Chlorophilia 2, 2015
Artemide, Pregnana Milanese, Italy

Moon jellyfish
Artemide, Pregnana Milanese, Italy

Ameluna, 2016
Artemide, Pregnana Milanese, Italy

Skeleton flower Diphylleia grayi
Alamy Stock Photo, alamy.de
Photographer: Little Dinosaur

Diphy, 2017
Linea Light Group, Castelminio di Resana, Italy

Rinspeed XchangE, 2014
Rinspeed, Zumikon, Switzerland

Volkswagen ID. ROOMZZ, 2019
Volkswagen AG, Wolfsburg, Germany

Audi A8 L, 2017
AUDI AG, Ingolstadt, Germany

Mercedes-Benz EQC, 2019
Daimler AG, Stuttgart, Germany

Porsche Macan S, 2018
Dr. Ing. h.c. F. Porsche AG, Stuttgart, Germany

Chapter | Kapitel
Form follows responsibility

TECTON LED strip light system, 2010
Zumtobel, Dornbirn, Austria

Daylight Greenhouse, 2014
Technokas, De Lier, The Netherlands

Despite careful research, it may be possible in exceptional cases that the copyright holders could not be identified or did not respond to requests. Compensation for justified claims will be made in accordance with standard agreements.

Trotz sorgfältiger Recherche kann es in Ausnahmefällen möglich sein, dass die Rechteinhaber nicht ermittelt werden konnten oder auf Anfragen nicht geantwortet haben. Berechtigte Ansprüche werden selbstverständlich im Rahmen der üblichen Vereinbarungen abgegolten.

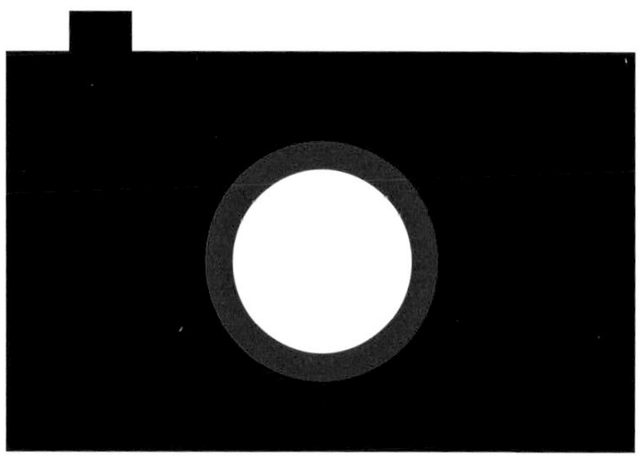

Imprint | Impressum

The Book of Possibilities –
Inspiring Design with PLEXIGLAS®
Red Dot Edition, August 2019

Concept | Konzept
Doris Hirsch, Profilwerkstatt,
Darmstadt, Germany
Burkhard Jacob, Red Dot Institute,
Essen, Germany

Editing & Research | Redaktion & Recherche
Doris Hirsch, Profilwerkstatt,
Darmstadt, Germany
Burkhard Jacob, Red Dot Institute,
Essen, Germany

Editorial Assistance | Redaktionelle Mitarbeit
Hannah Barthel, Profilwerkstatt,
Darmstadt, Germany
Olaf Hörning, Endegut, Eyendorf, Germany

Design Concept & Layout | Gestaltungskonzept & Layout
Endegut, Eyendorf, Germany

Illustrations | Illustrationen
Vera Hampe, Endegut, Eyendorf, Germany

Translation | Übersetzung
Kocarek, Essen, Germany
Tara Russell, Dublin, Ireland
Philippa Watts, Linguaphile, Exeter,
Great Britain
William Kings, Linguaphile, Wuppertal,
Germany

Copy Editing | Lektorat
Norbert Knyhala, Schmidt & Knyhala,
Castrop-Rauxel, Germany
Tara Russell, Dublin, Ireland
Philippa Watts, Linguaphile, Exeter,
Great Britain
William Kings, Linguaphile, Wuppertal,
Germany

Production | Produktion
Bernd Reinkens, gelb+, Düsseldorf,
Germany

Lithography | Lithografie
Bernd Reinkens (Supervision), gelb+,
Düsseldorf, Germany
Jonas Mühlenweg, Wurzel Medien,
Düsseldorf, Germany

Print | Druck
Gutenberg Beuys Feindruckerei GmbH
Hans-Böckler-Straße 52
30851 Langenhagen, Germany

Bookbinding | Buchbinderei
Integralis Industriebuchbinderei,
Lettershop & Fulfillment,
Hannover/Ronnenberg, Germany

This publication was realized in cooperation with
Siamak Djafarian
Vice President Molding Compounds Methacrylates
Röhm GmbH
Dolivostraße 17
64293 Darmstadt, Germany
Email plexiglas.polymers@roehm.com

RÖHM is a worldwide manufacturer of PMMA products sold under the PLEXIGLAS® and PLEXIMID® trademarks on the European, Asian, African and Australian continents and under the ACRYLITE® and ACRYMID® trademarks in the Americas.
PLEXIGLAS® and PLEXIMID® are registered trademarks of Röhm GmbH, Darmstadt, Germany.

RÖHM ist ein weltweiter Hersteller von PMMA-Produkten, die unter den Marken PLEXIGLAS® und PLEXIMID® auf dem europäischen, asiatischen, afrikanischen und australischen Kontinent vertrieben werden und unter den Marken ACRYLITE® und ACRYMID® auf dem amerikanischen Kontinent.
PLEXIGLAS® und PLEXIMID® sind registrierte Marken der Röhm GmbH, Darmstadt.

Publisher & Distribution | Verlag & Vertrieb
Red Dot GmbH & Co. KG
Gelsenkirchener Str. 181
45309 Essen, Germany
Book publisher ID no. | Verkehrsnummer
13674 (Börsenverein Frankfurt)

Red Dot Edition
Design Publisher | Fachbuchverlag für Design
Sabine Wöll
Phone +49 201 81418 22
Fax +49 201 81418 195
Email edition@red-dot.de

ISBN 978-3-89939-219-7

Bibliographic information published by the Deutsche Nationalbibliothek: The Deutsche Nationalbibliothek lists this publication in the Deutsche Nationalbibliografie; detailed bibliographic data are available on the Internet at http://dnb.ddb.de.

Bibliografische Information der Deutschen Nationalbibliothek: Die Deutsche Nationalbibliothek verzeichnet diese Publikation in der Deutschen Nationalbibliografie; detaillierte bibliografische Daten sind im Internet über http://dnb.ddb.de abrufbar.

reddot edition

CREATIVITY

Did PLEXIGLAS® inspire you? Here is room for your new ideas.

THE END